The Trail of Tears: The

By Charles River Editors

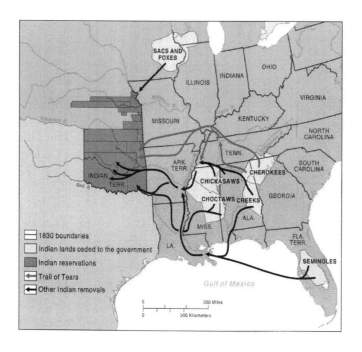

The forced removal of Native Americans in the Southeast

About Charles River Editors

Charles River Editors was founded by Harvard and MIT alumni to provide superior editing and original writing services, with the expertise to create digital content for publishers across a vast range of subject matter. In addition to providing original digital content for third party publishers, Charles River Editors republishes civilization's greatest literary works, bringing them to a new generation via ebooks.

Introduction

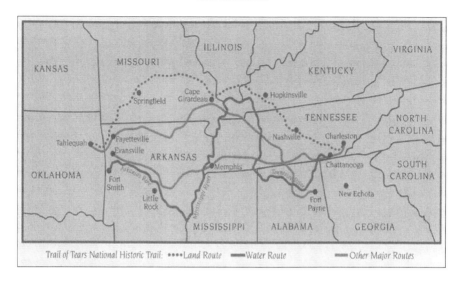

The Cherokee's routes during the Trail of Tears

The Trail of Tears

"I fought through the War Between the States and have seen many men shot, but the Cherokee Removal was the cruelest work I ever knew." – Georgia soldier on the Trail of Tears

The "Five Civilized Tribes" are among the best known Native American groups in American history, and they were even celebrated by contemporary Americans for their abilities to adapt to white culture. But tragically, they are also well known tribes due to the trials and tribulations they suffered by being forcibly moved west along the "Trail of Tears".

Though the Trail of Tears applied to several different tribes, it is most commonly associated today with the Cherokee. The Cherokee began the process of assimilation into European America very early, even before the establishment of the Unites States, but it is unclear what benefits that brought the tribe. Throughout the colonial period and after the American Revolution, the Cherokee struggled to satisfy the whims and desires of American government officials and settlers, often suffering injustices after complying with their desires. Nevertheless, the Cherokee continued to endure, and after being pushed west, they rose from humble origins as refugees new to the southeastern United States to build themselves back up into a powerhouse both economically and militarily. The Cherokee ultimately became the first people of non-European descent to become U.S. citizens en masse, and today the Cherokee Nation is the largest federally recognized tribe in the United States, boasting over 300,000 members.

The Creek became known as one of the Five Civilized Tribes for quickly assimilating aspects of European culture, but in response to early European contact, the Muscogee established one of the strongest confederacies in the region. Despite becoming a dominant regional force, however, infighting brought about civil war in the early 19th century, and they were quickly wrapped up in the War of 1812 as well. By the end of that fighting, the Creek were compelled to cede millions of acres of land to the expanding United States, ushering in a new era that found the Creek occupying only a small strip of Alabama by the 1830s.

With the Spanish Empire foundering during the mid-19th century, the young United States sought to take possession of Florida. President Andrew Jackson's notorious policy of Indian Removal led to the Seminole Wars in the 1830s, and that was already after General Andrew Jackson had led American soldiers against the Seminole in the First Seminole War a generation earlier. The Seminole Wars ultimately pushed much of the tribe into Oklahoma, and the nature of some of the fighting remains one of the best known aspects of Seminole history among Americans.

The Trail of Tears comprehensively covers the history and legacy of the events that brought about the removal of the Southeastern tribes. Along with pictures of important people, places, and events, you will learn about the Trail of Tears like you never have before, in no time at all.

The Trail of Tears: The History and Legacy of America's Infamous Indian Removal Policy

About Charles River Editors

Introduction

Chapter 1: Historical Origins of the Southeastern Tribes

Like many Native American tribes, the Cherokee experienced "forced migrations," both at the hands of their fellow indigenous people and most infamously during the Trail of Tears, when they were forced from their homeland by the U.S. military. As a result, the Cherokee are often associated with the Deep South, but originally, the Cherokee lived in the northeastern part of the present-day United States, around the Great Lakes. At some time in the distant past, the tribe was forced out of the region, probably at the hands of a militarily stronger tribe. While it has long been believed that it was the Iroquois who forced the Cherokee to migrate south and settle in the present-day southeastern United States. Delaware tribal legends support the defeat of the Cherokee but Iroquois legends make no mention of such a story.

Today it is believed that the Cherokee migrated south thousands of years ago. The Cherokee language is part of the Iroquoian language family but has changed significantly, indicating that the tribe left its ancestral homeland at least several millennia ago. Glottochronology is an anthropological technique of tracking linguistic changes in related languages to determine how long people groups sharing the root language have been separated. The technique studies core words and attempts to decipher the length of time needed to achieve perceived changes. Using this technique, researchers have estimated that the Cherokee departed from the Iroquois ancestors about 6,000 years ago. However, because language does not leave archaeological evidence, this estimate is far from certain.

The name Cherokee is likely derived from the Creek word chelokee, which means "people of a different speech." Also, though many Cherokee people accept the term "Cherokee," some prefer and use the word "Tsalagi" to refer to themselves and their tribe. Originally, the Cherokee referred to themselves as the Aniyunwiya or Anniyaya which can be translated as "the principal people. This moniker understandably fits with the Cherokee creation narrative, in which the Cherokee are the first (among many) Native American tribes to occupy the Earth. They also called themselves the Keetoowah, meaning the "people of Kituhwa." Other indigenous tribes had names for the Cherokee, many of which resemble Cherokee, Tsalagi, and Keetoohwa. A few examples are: Chilukki (used by the Choctaw and Chickasaw and meaning "dog people"), Talligewi (used by the Delaware people), and Kittuwa (used by the Algonquin people).

From their northeastern origins, the Cherokee migrated to the present-day southeastern United States to settle in a region currently composed of parts of western North and South Carolina, Northern Georgia, southwestern Virginia, and the Cumberland Basin of Tennessee, Kentucky, and northern Alabama. While the tribe's population prior to European contact remains unknown, it is estimated that epidemics beginning in 1540 (the date of first contact with the DeSoto Expedition) likely killed at least 75% of the tribe's population. By 1674, the Cherokee had rebounded to about 50,000 members, but a series of epidemics in 1729, 1738, and 1753 further reduced this number by half. Just prior to their removal in the late 1830s, the population was around 25,000 and relatively stable.

The Cherokee tribe has traditionally been divided into three sub-groups based upon location and the distinct dialect of the Cherokee language. The Lower Cherokee lived in the eastern-most villages, and the Over-the-Hill Cherokee were those who occupied the western-most towns. As their designation implies, the Middle Cherokee occupied the territory between the two aforementioned groups. In addition to these three groups, several other distinctive bands of Cherokee people are identified as the Chickamauga, Onnontiogg, and Qualia. Also identified are two bands – the Atali and the Etali – whose names suggest that they may be one band that was given two different names by those who recorded them.

According to Creek oral tradition, the Creek people migrated to the U. S. Southeast from west of the Mississippi River before ultimately settling in Alabama and Georgia. It had long been believed that the "Creek" designation came from the English due to men like historian-trader James Adair, who in the early 18th century observed, "Most [Creek] towns are very commodiously and pleasantly situated on large beautiful creeks or rivers where the lands are fertile, the waters clean and well tasted, and the air extremely pure"[1]. However, modern scholarship cites a more specific origin for the use of the name Creek, arguing that it is a colloquial reference to the Muskogean-speaking Ochesee culture, who lived along the Ocmulgee River (in Georgia) in the 1600s and were referred to by traders as "Ochesee of the Creek" or "Creek." Ironically, scholars believe the Ochesee, who may have been responsible for the use of the term Creek to refer to so many groups, were never actually part of mainstream Muskogean society.

Oral tradition does not detail their cultural progress, but most anthropologists view the original ancestors of the Muskogee/Creek (or ProtoMuskogee/Creek) as a melding of various religious and cultural "Moundbuilding" traditions, including Hopewellian and Mississippian, which they practiced in a relatively uniform manner until dividing themselves. The Muskogee occupying the lower half of the occupational area became the "Lower" Muskogee and later the Lower Creek, while those in the northern area became the "Upper" Muskogee and later Upper Creek. According to one theory, it was the array of new diseases introduced by Europeans, for which the indigenous population of North American had no immunity, that ultimately led to the collapse of the Prehistoric Mississippian Culture and sent indigenous populations fleeing east. After regrouping with other Muskogean-speaking relatives occupying the region, they formed the ProtoMuskogee Nation, also referred to as a Confederacy.

While the date of first European contact cannot be provided with certainty, Spanish explorers of the mid-1500s wrote of encountering indigenous groups occupying mound-based communities in the South Carolina-Florida-Alabama tri-state area that fit the Muskogee/Creek description. By

---

[1] *Green, Donald E.* The Creek People. *Page 4.*

this time, several Muskogee groups had consolidated into a sizable Confederacy to resist outside influence. Scattered into more than 50 agricultural hamlets known as *idalwas* ("Creek towns" to the English), many of which had more than 1,000 inhabitants, the "Confederacy" grew exponentially as European settlement displaced other indigenous groups and their members sought protection under the Muskogee/Creek.

While the earliest history of the Seminole in Florida is still not well understood, it is commonly accepted that the first group to venture into the state were the Apalache, an Hitchiti-speaking people believed to be related to the Tamathli or Appalachicola Creek. Interestingly, the Seminole Nation of Oklahoma regard the Oconee as the original "Seminole", a group which later included the Hecete, Eufaula, Mikasuki, Horrewahle, Tallahassee, Chiaha, and Appalachicola. While members of numerous other Muscogee bands soon followed, it was the Apalache (camped along the Apalachicola River) who first came into contact with Spanish explorers. And although an attempt by the Spanish to set up a system of missions across north Florida and southern Georgia in the 16th century ultimately failed, it did succeed in drawing various Creek from Georgia into Florida.

When Spain first settled the North American peninsula, they named it Florida. Pedro Menéndez de Avilés founded St. Augustine in 1565, the first permanent settlement in Florida after at least 60 years of Spanish exploration, and during that time he reported discovery of Native American groups from three different language groups (the Timuquan, Calusan, and Muskhogean) occupying the land. The Native Americans lived in small, well-organized villages sustained by farming, fishing, hunting, and raising livestock. According to most modern historians, the majority of those encountered at this time were actually the Apalache, an Hitchiti-speaking people believed to be related to the Tamathli or Apalachicola Creek.

In the second half of the 18th century, the British took Florida from the Spanish, and the Seminole embedded themselves deeper into the interior of Florida, where it was safer among the jungles and swamps. The Seminole also took in many escaped slaves, who found safe haven among the tribe. In 1763, a Royal British Proclamation decreed that land would be set aside specifically for use by various Native American groups. The British restricted white settlement to "Crown-claimed" lands east of the Appalachian Mountains. This designation remained until the Treaty of Paris ended the American Revolution in 1783 and ceded the land to the newly-formed United States. In fact, up until the time of the American Revolution, the indigenous people of the Southeast had maintained a relatively non-contentious relationship with the British, and many even swore loyalty to the British Empire.

After the British defeat, however, the new American government began an aggressive campaign to claim Native American lands, exemplified by the Battle of Fallen Timbers in 1794, which resulted in the government taking Native American lands in Ohio and Indiana. This led to various areas of the east still occupied by Native Americans being referred to as "Indian

Country". Some of these areas were established by treaties, but some of them existed simply because they hadn't been confronted by American settlers and soldiers.

Around 1760 what is thought to have been the first permanent Creek/Seminole settlement was established at Chocuchattee ("red house") near present-day Brooksville, Florida, where the Creek (who the Spanish called *Seminole*, meaning "the runaways" or by some reckoning, "free people") raised cattle. And though even half a century later (by the time of the War of 1812) the Seminole population remained relatively small--around 1200 as compared to the Creeks of Georgia and Alabama whose numbers may have exceeded 25,000—the growing White population had grown increasingly leery of their presence.

Chapter 2: The Cherokee and Europeans

Hernando de Soto

The first contact with Cherokee people made by Europeans occurred in 1540, when members of the de Soto Expedition recorded that they had found "Chalaque" settlements along the Tennessee River. The Spanish established and maintained a small mining and smelting operation that remained in the region until around 1690, but because the Cherokee generally lived in remote mountainous regions, they were able to avoid frequent contact with European settlers until about 1609, when the colony of Virginia was established.

By 1629, English settlers had entered the Appalachian Mountains and came into contact with Cherokee villages, and after the founding of the Carolina colonies, European contact with the

Cherokee became almost constant. An expedition sent by Virginia-based trader Abraham Wood established a trading network with Cherokee living in their capital at Echota in present-day northern Alabama in 1673. Though Virginia traders attempted to maintain a monopoly on the lucrative trade in animal skins and Native American slaves with the Cherokee, the enterprising indigenous group approached newcomers from the Carolinas and established trade connections with them the following year as well. Traders from South Carolina established a treaty with Cherokee living in their area by 1684, and a steady flow of deerskins and slaves began to flow out of the Cherokee villages.

During this time, life among the Cherokee inevitably began to change as well. As contact with colonial traders increased, the level of dependence on European goods increased among the Cherokee. Moreover, the political power base within the Cherokee settlements shifted from the priest/shaman class to that of the hunter/warrior as the latter became "hunters for profit." The increasing reliance on European goods from the English colonies also caused the Cherokee to ally themselves with the English against the Spanish and French during conflicts between 1689 and 1763. This was a natural byproduct of the fact that Cherokee warriors raided Spanish settlements in present-day northern Florida in the 1670s, and they were also fighting with the coastal tribes in the Carolinas.

The frequent warring between the Native American tribes was exacerbated by the fact that the Europeans introduced superior military technology to them upon their arrival. By 1680, most tribes in the region had acquired firearms, forcing the larger Cherokee settlements throughout the region to become more militarized and fortified against attack. Also during this period, conflicts with the Catawba to the east and the Choctaw and Creek to the south escalated until the tribes were engaged in almost constant fighting. Traditional enmity with the Chickasaw, another Native American tribe allied with the British, also kept the Cherokee busy with fighting to the west. On top of all that, there were territory conflicts along the northern frontiers of Cherokee territory between English, French, and Dutch traders.

While the Cherokee fought their traditional enemies and the European conflict evolved into the Beaver Wars, the expanding and powerful Iroquois League pushed Native Americans out of the Great Lakes, creating a stream of refugees that headed south and also came into contact with the Cherokee. As a result, during the mid-17th century, large numbers of Shawnee people were forced out of their traditional homelands by powerful Iroquois bands, and these refugees entered traditionally Cherokee territory. Taking advantage of the situation and essentially using the Shawnee as a buffer, the Cherokee allowed the refugees to settle between themselves and their regional enemies. One Shawnee group was allowed to settle in South Carolina between Cherokee towns and the Catawba tribe, and a second group was allowed to settle in the Cumberland Basin of Tennessee as a buffer between the Cherokee and the Chickasaw.

This decision eventually proved problematic for the Cherokee when the Iroquois, remembering their enemies, ventured south and raided Shawnee and Cherokee settlements. Eventually, the Shawnee grew into a threat to the Cherokee as well, and in the late 17th century, Shawnee raiders destroyed a major Cherokee town while raiding it for slaves because the village's warriors were away on a hunt. The raid destroyed the fragile trust that had existed between the Cherokee and Shawnee, and the following year a group of Cherokee leaders traveled to Charlestown and asked for additional firearms to defend their villages against raiders bent on capturing slaves for the lucrative South Carolina trade.

Attitudes among the Cherokee in the Carolinas were so dangerously inflammatory that during the first decade of the 18th century, North Carolina officials demanded that South Carolina traders curtail the Native American slave trade for fear of a general rebellion. British government officials eventually stepped in and brokered a peace treaty between the Iroquois and the Cherokee, and over the course of the next 10 years, Cherokee warriors allied with different partners – both colonials and fellow Native American tribes – to secure their region and rid themselves of common enemies. Still, the Shawnee problem remained, and in 1715 Cherokee warriors entered into an alliance with their old adversaries, the Chickasaw. Together, the two tribes dealt a crippling blow to the Shawnee in the Cumberland Basin, but their alliance attracted the attention of both the French traders and their Algonquin allies, who began a series of raids against Cherokee villages from strongholds north of the Ohio River.

This period of conflict would last until the middle of the 18th century, during which time the Cherokee found themselves fighting Native American allies of both the British (the Iroquois) and the French (the Algonquins). Finally, in 1745, the Cherokee again allied with the Chickasaw and drove the remaining Shawnee over the Ohio River and out of Cherokee territory for good. The alliance then turned on another common enemy and French ally, the Choctaw, and defeated them in 1750.

The first half of the 18th century also saw the first land ceded to white settlers by the Cherokee. In a treaty between British colonists and Cherokee tribal members in 1721, a boundary between Cherokee and British settlements was established, but North Carolina and South Carolina settlers were soon making incursions into Lower Cherokee territory east of the Appalachians anyway. Additionally, French traders had established a trading post near Montgomery, Alabama in 1717 and made contact with the Over-the-Hill Cherokee by navigating along the Cumberland River. Many Cherokee were tempted to switch their allegiance from the British to the French, but practical realities dissuaded them. French goods were of lower quality than those provided by the British, and the British had the naval power to effectively cut off French colonies in Canada by blockading the northeast points of entry. Also, the Chickasaw made navigation on the Tennessee River, a major trading route, virtually impossible for the French.

The British, sensing that the Cherokee might be tempted by French offers of allegiance, sent representatives to regulate trade and streamline trade relations by urging the Cherokee to appoint a single chief for each town, and British influence also led to peace treaties between the Cherokee and their former enemies the Catawba and the Wyandot tribes. During these peace negotiations, the Cherokee learned that the Wyandot and other Native American tribes were secretly planning to abandon their trade alliances with the French, information that ended any further consideration of the French as a trade alternative to the British. In the end, the French were simply unable to compete with the British in terms of quality of goods and access to Native American trading partners.

At the same time, the British remained concerned that the Cherokee would switch alliances, and they weren't entirely concerned about maintaining their end of the land bargains they struck with the Cherokee. Throughout the remainder of the 18th century, the Cherokee lost land to British colonists invading and settling on their land, and the tribe alternated between fighting against them and for them.

During the American Revolution, the Cherokee sided with the British, and the decision cost them heavily. Cherokee war parties engaged in several unsuccessful raids against American settlements, and the colonists responded with several victories, forcing the Cherokee to sue for peace. In the ensuing peace negotiations, the Cherokee gave up their ancestral and historical claims to territory in North Carolina and South Carolina, codified in the Treaty of DeWitts Corner (1777) and the Treaties of Long Island of Holston drafted in 1777 and 1781. The defeats and the territorial concessions would induce the Cherokee to strive for assimilation into American society in the early 19th century.

By the early 19th century, the Cherokee had actively begun trying to assimilate into U.S. society, the most notable byproduct of which was their written constitution (which can be found in the appendix). In their constitution, the tribe codified its governmental system and established both court and school systems. Many members of the tribe also converted to Christianity, and white missionaries lived among them unhindered. In fact, the tribe's rapid advancement and relative affluence made their white neighbors envious of the Cherokee's standard of living.

In 1821, Sequoyah (also known as George Gist) developed a writing system for the Cherokee language. Using a system of 86 symbols, each with a phonetic value, Sequoyah assigned syllabic values to each symbol that represented all the sounds used while speaking the Cherokee language. Because the system was relatively simple and easy to learn, the vast majority of Cherokee people became literate in their native tongue within a few years. Furthermore, *The Phoenix*, a Cherokee language newspaper, began publication in February 1828. Due to these early efforts to assimilate into U.S. society and adopt practices, the Cherokee remain one of the most highly educated Native American tribes and maintain one of the highest standards of living among indigenous peoples.

A lithograph based off a portrait of Sequoya

Chapter 3: Creek Conflicts with Europeans and Americans

Throughout the 17th century, the Upper Creek numbers were increased considerably by Shawnee who had relocated to South Carolina and then Alabama to fulfill trade and alliance obligations, and by the late 17th and early 18th centuries, the Creek had allied with the Spanish, French, and British at one point or another, acquiring horses and guns in the process. That said, the alliances were often different between the Upper Creek and Lower Creek, and the Spanish, French, and British alliances were routinely formed with Creek splinter groups hired as mercenaries. This caused schisms among the Confederacy, and the Creek quickly found themselves caught in a three-way crossfire among European rivals. The Spanish controlled the area south of the Creek Nation, the French had established a stronghold at Mobile Bay, Alabama, and the English had imposed their rule on the area east of the Savannah River, which formed most of the border between South Carolina and Georgia.

The first permanent white settlement on Creek Confederation land was established in 1733 when General James Oglethorpe, a philanthropist and Member of British Parliament, formed the Georgia Colony along the banks of the Savannah River, erecting numerous buildings and setting in crops. Though many Creek worried about inviting invasion, a short time later Chief

Tomochichi approved the founding of the town of Savannah at the eastern edge of Creek territory.

Portrait of Oglethorpe

Depiction of Tomochichi and a nephew holding an eagle

Tomochichi was the first Creek leader to gain notoriety among the Europeans, and as chief of the Yamacraw (of the Lower Creek), he served as the principal mediator between the native population and English settlers during the first years of settlement. He was ultimately credited with helping establish amicable relations between the two groups, as well as the success of the founding of the state of Georgia. Around 1728, *Tomochichi* had created his own Yamacraw tribe from an assortment of Creek and Yamasee after the two nations disagreed over future relations with the English and Spanish, ultimately forming a group of approximately 200 who settled on the bluffs of the Savannah River.

In 1734 Tomochichi accompanied General James Oglethorpe to England, along with a small delegation of Lower Creek members, and while in England he acted as mediator during numerous meetings with various English dignitaries. Upon his return to Georgia, Tomochichi met with other Lower Creek chiefs to assure them of the honest intentions of the English, thereby convincing them to ally with the English despite previous deceitful encounters with their neighbors in South Carolina. In turn, during the summer of 1739, Oglethorpe made an unprecedented visit to the Creek town of Coweta to bolster his connection with the Lower Creek, resulting in what was considered a mutually favorable treaty. Tomochichi, however, was unable to participate in the negotiations, because he was forced to remain in his village with a serious illness. On October 5, 1739, Tomochichi died.

After the French and Indian War, the British had emerged as the dominant European force in North America, and English traders capitalized on their standing by establishing trade with the Creek, introducing such items as steel knives, iron pots, cotton cloth, and more guns. This relationship would add new stressors to Creek society because they became less self-reliant and more dependent on British trade. During the American Revolution, both the Upper and Lower Creek remained fundamentally neutral and didn't want to take sides, but as the American colonists attempted to establish friendly relations through trade, the British made trade contingent upon loyalty. Ultimately, Creek loyalty was decided by Alexander McGillivray, a member of the prestigious and powerful Wind Clan.

Alexander McGillivray was a controversial Creek leader born to Scottish trader Lachlan McGillivray and a Creek woman named Sehoy, and he grew up as a full member of his mother's Wind Clan. Before joining Creek society in 1777, McGillivray had lived in Augusta, Georgia, received a typical white education in Charleston, South Carolina, and had a business apprenticeship in Savannah, Georgia. Upon arriving in the Creek Nation, McGillivray quickly realized that his multi-lingual abilities and inherent understanding of Creek and white societies gave him unique abilities and insight that were invaluable to the Creek.

After accepting a commission as a colonel in the Royal British Army during the Revolutionary War, McGillivray worked for British Superintendent of Indian Affairs John Stuart. At the behest of Upper Creek chief Emistesguo, McGillivray accepted the position of Principal Chief of the Creek Nation, subsequently orchestrating alliances between Creek and British forces in 1778. After the signing of the Treaty of Paris in 1783, however, the Creek watched as their British allies evacuated the region, exposing their frontier to American settlement.

McGillivray was stripped of his diplomatic negotiating power, but in 1790 he led a delegation of Creek to New York City to negotiate with President George Washington, resulting in the Treaty of New York. In this treaty, the federal government promised to defend Creek Nation territorial rights, and it established a formal relationship between the United States and the Creek. It also affirmed McGillivray's position as a legitimate potentate and leader, but just three years later, McGillivray died in Pensacola, Florida at the age of 43.

In 1795, the federal government implemented the first of George Washington's policies designed to "civilize" the native population by transforming them into farmers. Unlike the majority of indigenous groups who demonstrated no natural propensity for full-time farming, the Creek were highly successful agriculturalists already. The Americans supplied the Creek peoples with iron plows and blacksmiths to maintain them, a policy that initially proved productive, but the Indian Agents urged them to establish traditional farms away from Creek *idalwas*. They accomplished this by supplying livestock, cotton seed, and spinning wheels, and by 1800, major *idalwas* like Coweta were practically ghost-towns. Still, even after the demise of most traditional Creek towns, the surrounding Creek continued to use the old squares for ritual and celebrations.

In many ways, the abandonment of the original Creek *idalwas* spelled the beginning of the end of traditional Creek life. After the signing of the Treaty of New York in 1790, the Treaty of Colerain in 1796, the Treaty of Fort Wilkinson in 1802, and the Treaty of Washington in 1805, by 1810 the trail blazed across Creek land had cut the Creek Nation in two, leaving it unprotected from white settlers' intrusion. With that, the westward pushing settlers pressured the government and demanded protection, asking that the Native Americans be controlled so the settlers could safely live on the land. frontier settlers demanding the "Indians" be taken under control so they could take prime land for settlement,

With that, many Native Americans sought to unify various tribes into a coordinated resistance. The most famous of these efforts was led by the Shawnee chief, Tecumseh. Tecumseh's influence increased as he advocated a rising Native American religious movement, led by his brother Tenskwatawa. Initially known as Lalawethika, he was born after his father Puckshinwa's death at the Battle of Point Pleasant (1794), Lalawethika was also soon abandoned by his mother, leaving him an orphan. He never learned the vital warrior skills of hunting and fighting and also lost an eye in a hunting accident. Quickly becoming a wayward soul lost in the cracks of his tribal society, Lalawethika was prone to heavy drinking and was known by other Native Americans as a braggart, with his poor looks and behavior resulting in him growing up as an outsider.

19th century depiction of Tecumseh

One night, while heavily under the influence of alcohol, he fell into a fire and was thought to have died, but he unexpectedly awoke and told of a vision he'd received from the *Master of Life*, the Algonquin title for "god" (the Shawnee shared the Algonquin language group and likely their foundational religious beliefs). After this vision, Lalawethika changed his name to Tenskwatawa (the Open Door or One with Open Mouth) and began preaching.

Portrait depicting Tenskwatawa by George Catlin.

The new holy man experienced a series of visions that greatly changed his life and led him to abandon his old ways. He led a purification movement and exhorted Native Americans to separate themselves from whites and return to the ways of their ancestors, forbidding his followers from using alcohol and any European foods, clothing, or manufactured goods. With his popularity and following growing, Tenskwatawa founded a settlement for his small group of followers near present-day Greenville, Ohio, where he preached that the white settlers were the spawn of the "Great Serpent", which according to Algonquin tradition came from the sea and stood for evil powers. *The Prophet*, as Tenskwatawa became known, was a follower of Delaware holy men who had died years early but had predicted that the white men would be overthrown by supernatural powers. This apocalyptic theology was a precursor for the Ghost Dance movement that would rise among Native Americans of the Great Plains and Southwest near the end of the nineteenth century. When the Delaware (Lenape) chief Buckongahelas died of either influenza or small pox during 1805, Tenskwatawa declared it an act of witchcraft and began a witch-hunt, which resulted in the deaths of several Delaware "witches."

As Tenskwatawa's movement grew, settlers and military officials in the region became concerned about the Prophet's growing influence among the area's Native Americans. In 1806, William Henry Harrison began to publicly denounce Tenskwatawa to other tribal leaders, calling him a fraud and charlatan. The Shawnee Prophet responded by accurately predicting a solar eclipse, which embarrassed Governor Harrison, and after this event, which tribal leaders took as a sign of Tenskwatawa's authenticity, his movement grew even more rapidly. By 1808, Tenskwatawa and his followers had moved west and founded a large, multi-tribal settlement near the confluence of the Tippecanoe and Wabash Rivers, called Prophetstown or Tippecanoe. Assisted by his brother Tecumseh, Tenskwatawa's settlement grew tremendously and eventually became the largest Native American settlement in the region. It also served as a Native American cultural center and provided a steady cadre of warriors ready to hear the Prophet's message that they should return to their ancestral lifestyles and force the white settlers and their culture out of their territory.

In addition to its political and military importance, the Prophetstown settlement was spiritually important and advantageously located (probably on purpose) at the confluence of two rivers, a place of strong spiritual significance for Native Americans. Tenskwatawa's movement was fundamentally a spiritual one, based on purification of both Native American culture and society and the land itself – and by ejecting the American influence. At its peak, some 3,000 Native Americans lived at Prophetstown.

Meanwhile, Tecumseh, who was increasingly seen as a leader among the Shawnee and other Native Americans, began to travel around the lower Great Lakes region in 1808, visiting Native

American leaders and using his considerable rhetorical and oratorical skills to urge them to stop cooperating with invading Americans and threatening to kill those leaders who continued to do so. After the signing of the Treaty of Fort Wayne in 1809, Tecumseh warned Native American leaders who had signed the treaty that those who attempted to carry out the terms would be killed.

The real goal for Tecumseh was to convince Native Americans to unite in a multi-tribal confederacy strong enough to halt westward expansion by settlers. Numerous tribal leaders agreed to join Tecumseh's confederacy, but even those who did not lost warriors and families to the Prophetstown settlement. It's believed that in 1808, Tecumseh had about 5,000 warriors at his disposal, scattered about the region in villages or at Prophetstown, and that same year the British in Canada approached the leader hoping to form an alliance. The British and U.S. had seen their own tensions rise over issues like trade and the British impressments of American sailors, and they would fight the War of 1812 a few years later. At this time, however, Tecumseh refused the offer and gradually grew to become the leader of the confederacy, much of which was built upon the religious appeal of his brother's purification movement.

As he tried to find allies among the Five Civilized Tribes, Tecumseh also gave an impassioned war speech in October 1811 during a meeting with the Muscogee Creek, the tribe his father was believed to have belonged to:

"In defiance of the white warriors of Ohio and Kentucky, I have traveled through their settlements, once our favorite hunting grounds. No war-whoop was sounded, but there is blood on our knives. The Pale-faces felt the blow, but knew not whence it came. Accursed be the race that has seized on our country and made women of our warriors. Our fathers, from their tombs, reproach us as slaves and cowards. I hear them now in the wailing winds. The Muscogee was once a mighty people. The Georgians trembled at your war-whoop, and the maidens of my tribe, on the distant lakes, sung the prowess of your warriors and sighed for their embraces. Now your very blood is white; your tomahawks have no edge; your bows and arrows were buried with your fathers. Oh! Muscogees, brethren of my mother, brush from your eyelids the sleep of slavery; once more strike for vengeance; once more for your country. The spirits of the mighty dead complain. Their tears drop from the weeping skies. Let the white race perish. They seize your land; they corrupt your women; they trample on the ashes of your dead! Back, whence they came, upon a trail of blood, they must be driven. Back! back, ay, into the great water whose accursed waves brought them to our shores! Burn their dwellings! Destroy their stock! Slay their wives and children! The Red Man owns the country, and the Pale-faces must never enjoy it. War now! War forever! War upon the living! War upon the dead! Dig their very corpses from the grave. Our country must give no rest to a white man's bones. This is the will of the Great Spirit, revealed to my brother, his familiar, the Prophet of the Lakes. He sends me to you. All the tribes of the north are dancing the war-dance. Two mighty warriors across the seas will send us arms. Tecumseh will soon return to his country. My prophets shall tarry with you. They will stand between you and the bullets of your enemies. When the white men approach you the yawning earth shall swallow them up. Soon shall you see my arm of fire stretched athwart the sky. I will stamp my foot at Tippecanoe, and the very earth shall shake."

Despite Tecumseh's pleas, most of the southern tribes refused Tecumseh's offers. Choctaw Chief Pushmataha countered Tecumseh by claiming coexistence was possible and advocated abiding by the terms of the treaties: "These white Americans ... give us fair exchange, their cloth, their guns, their tools, implements, and other things which the Choctaws need but do not make ... So in marked contrast with the experience of the Shawnee, it will be seen that the whites and Indians in this section are living on friendly and mutually beneficial terms."

Portrait of Pushmataha

Only a faction (Upper Creek) of the Creek Nation, called the Red Sticks, responded to Tecumseh's call for violent resistance. Like Tecumseh, the Red Sticks had seen their brethren among the Lower Creek make land cessions in their ancestral homelands (modern Georgia) in 1790, 1802, and 1805. As invading American settlers ruined the hunting grounds, the Lower Creek were forced to adopt the American, agricultural lifestyle and had forsaken many of their traditions. The younger men from the Upper Creek villages had been agitating for a return to traditional cultural and spiritual lifestyles, and Tenskwatawa's purification movement appealed to these village leaders and was heavily influential in their decisions to resist. Their response eventually blossomed into the Creek War or Red Stick War during 1813 and 1814.

Tensions ignited in 1812 when a group of pro-Tecumseh Creek attacked and killed white settlers in the north country. Conditions then escalated when Menawa and William McIntosh, Principal Chiefs of the Upper and Lower Creek respectively, each dispatched a force to punish those Creek guilty and circumvent any further hostilities. Although they succeeded in killing those guilty, the "Red Sticks" retaliated, waging war against the resistant Creek. A short time later, Menawa joined the "Red Sticks" faction, and William McIntosh, now the leader of what was regarded by Americans as the "Loyal Creek" faction, was commissioned into the U. S. Army. Even when fighting amongst themselves, the Creek were embroiled in a war involving whites.

In late August 1813, the "Red Sticks" under William Weatherford, also known as *Lumhe Chati* ("Red Eagle"), attacked and destroyed the Upper Creek stronghold of Tuckabatchee, as well as a number of other Creek towns. As survivors quickly raced to take refuge among their Lower Creek cousins, Weatherford then led his warriors south, attacking Fort Mims near modern-day Mobile, Alabama, where they killed several hundred soldiers and white settlers. As word spread that the Upper Creek were on the "war path," Adjutant-General of the Tennessee Militia Andrew Jackson raised a volunteer army of Creek, Choctaw, and Cherokee to stop the violence. As Jackson's army attacked from the north, Federal troops attacked from the south, and the Georgia militia joined in from the east. The entire Creek Nation was surrounded and essentially laid to waste.

On March 27, 1814, the combined Georgia and Alabama militias attacked the "Red Stick" stronghold at Horseshoe Bend on the Tallapoosa River in Alabama. In the ensuing battle, Jackson's forces killed more than 500 Red Sticks, with Principal Chief Menawa severely wounded among them. Although Menawa managed to escape, both he and William Weatherford would surrender a few weeks later, as did all the Creek who did not flee to Florida to join their Seminole cousins.

Red Eagle (Weatherford) surrendering to Jackson after the Battle of Horseshoe Bend

When hostilities finally ceased, Andrew Jackson called a council of all the Creek Nation leaders at Fort Jackson, South Carolina to decide their fate. Though confident they would be fairly compensated for fighting the "Red Sticks" and helping the federal government secure peace in the region, Jackson instead demanded they cede 22 million acres of land bordering Florida to the U. S., offering no compensation whatsoever other than being deemed "loyal" Creeks who would be looked upon favorably in the future. According to the language of the Treaty, the federal government had taken this view: "Whereas an unprovoked, inhuman, and sanguinary war, waged by the hostile Creeks against the United States, hath been repelled, prosecuted and determined, successfully, on the part of the said States, in conformity with principles of national justice and honorable warfare. And whereas consideration is due to the rectitude of proceeding dictated by instructions relating to the re-establishment of peace: Be it remembered, that prior to the conquest of that part of the Creek nation hostile to the United States, numberless aggressions had been committed against the peace, the property, and the lives of citizens of the United States."[2] In essence, the Creek were being held responsible for others rebelling on their land.

---

[2] *First People website, "Treaties and Agreement."*

Ultimately, for damages sustained in fighting the "Red Stick" faction, the Lower Creek were awarded $195,000; $85,000 of which was paid in 1817. The remainder was not paid until 1853, when the dollar had been greatly devalued. The government would then sell Creek land to settlers at a profit of more than $11 million.

Chapter 4: Cherokee Nation v. Georgia

"I rejoice, brothers, to hear you propose to become cultivators of the earth for the maintenance of your families. Be assured you will support them better and with less labor, by raising stock and bread, and by spinning and weaving clothes, than by hunting. A little land cultivated, and a little labor, will procure more provisions than the most successful hunt; and a woman will clothe more by spinning and weaving, than a man by hunting. Compared with you, we are but as of yesterday in this land. Yet see how much more we have multiplied by industry, and the exercise of that reason which you possess in common with us. Follow then our example, brethren, and we will aid you with great pleasure."[3] – Thomas Jefferson, 1803

Independence from the British during the Revolutionary War merely confirmed to the Founders that the racial problems on the frontier would persist and create more violence. Fighting with the Cherokee continued after independence, as more and more American settlers crossed the Appalachian mountains to colonize their perceived "national inheritance":

"From the very beginning of United State's policy toward the Indians, missionaries (as well as government agents) played a critical role in the civilization/christianization of the indigenous inhabitants of North America. George Washington's Indian policy stated that 'missionaries of excellent moral character should be appointed to reside in their nation who should be well supplied with all the implements of husbandry and the necessary stock for a model farm.' It went further to state 'It is particularly important that something of this nature should be attempted with the Southern nations of Indians, whose confined situation might render them proper subjects for the experiment.' With the establishment of the first model farms and missions among the Five Civilized Tribes of the Southeastern United States, a key element in this civilization process was the implementation of African slaves as laborers in the building and operation of the model farms and missions."[4]

Despite their determined and legitimate attempts at assimilation, the Cherokee were ultimately forced to surrender their ancestral lands as white settlers pushed west. While President Andrew

---

[3] Jefferson's Indian Addresses, "To the Brothers of the Choctaw Nation, December 17, 1803," http://avalon.law.yale.edu/19th_century/jeffind3.asp

[4] U.S. Data Repository, "Beneath the Underdog: Race, Religion, and the Trail of Tears," http://www.us-data.org/us/minges/underdog.html

Jackson framed the removal of Cherokee people from their land as necessary for the advancement of the nation, nothing the Cherokee could do seemed enough to satisfy the United States government. The tribe had done everything asked of it, including changing its lifestyle, appointing a principal chief, and achieving widespread conversion to Christianity, but it would not be enough.

Of all the forced relocations of Native Americans during the 19th century and the various wars fought between the U.S. Army and native tribes, the relocation of the Cherokee remains the best known in American history. Even before the "Trail of Tears", many Cherokees had moved west and north to places like present-day Arkansas, Missouri and Texas to avoid the hostilities between the Cherokee, British, and other tribes. This was especially the case during the American Revolution, during which Cherokee, Choctaw and Chickasaw all began to voluntarily move west to avoid the conflict. Ironically, by the time the U.S. government signed the Treaty of St. Louis with the Osage in 1825, they claimed the Osage had to "cede and relinquish to the United States, all their right, title, interest, and claim, to lands lying within the State of Missouri and Territory of Arkansas" so the Cherokees and Creeks could reside there.

The Cherokee's troubles began in earnest at the beginning of the 19th century, when the U.S. government settled a territorial dispute between the states of Georgia, Alabama and Mississippi that required not recognizing the Cherokee's possession of lands claimed by Georgia. At first, the government tried to induce the Cherokee to move voluntarily off this land by creating a new reservation in Arkansas during the 1810s. The Cherokees who did head west to that reservation would ultimately become known as "old settlers", indicative of what was going to follow them.

This fracturing of the Cherokee tribe ahead of the Trail of Tears can be attributed to their contact with white settlers, which caused factions to form with the tribe. The differences among the Cherokee were illustrated and defined by the three distinct courses of action each advocated for. One group sought complete assimilation with the United States; a second group sought to adopt some aspects of American culture while remaining a separate and distinct nation; and the third faction advocated for maintaining the tribe as a separate entity and reverting to a traditional way of life. The threat of forced removal caused conflict between the leaders of these factions and disparate responses from the various groups. Most importantly, these differing attitudes towards assimilation with the United States resulted in the Trail of Tears affecting the tribe in several different ways. In addition to those who would die as a direct result of the removal, the Cherokee Nation itself was divided and fractured into bands that settled in several different places. Finally, those Cherokee who completed the journey to "Indian Territory" experienced severe political and cultural conflicts as the tribe settled in this new land and attempted to reestablish its previously well-ordered society.

After gold was discovered in Georgia on Cherokee land in 1828, the state passed a series of laws severely restricting Cherokee rights in Georgia. These laws also authorized the forced removal of Cherokee people from their historic territory. In an attempt to defend their rights to the land, Cherokee representatives cited previous treaties, arguing that the treaties had been negotiated between the Cherokee Nation (a separate and sovereign entity) and the United States. The tribe formed a delegation led by the principal Chief John Ross, and the delegation traveled to Washington D.C. to appeal to President Andrew Jackson and the Congress.

Chief John Ross

When these negotiations failed, the Cherokee sought an injunction to halt the imposition of the repressive Georgia laws. The initial case, *Cherokee Nation v. Georgia* (1831), was heard before the Supreme Court, but though the Court sympathized with the Cherokee's problem, it was dismissed when the Court ruled that it did not have jurisdiction to hear the case. Although the Constitution authorized the Supreme Court to hear cases involving "foreign nations", the Court held that "foreign nations" could not be applied to "Indian nations." In one of the most famous (and shortest) Supreme Court cases in American history, Chief Justice John Marshall wrote:

"MARSHALL, C. J. This bill is brought by the Cherokee nation, praying an injunction to restrain the state of Georgia from the execution of certain laws of that state, which, as is alleged, go directly to annihilate the Cherokee as a political society, and to seize for the use of Georgia, the lands of the nation which have been assured to them by the United States, in solemn treaties repeatedly made and still in force.

If courts were permitted to indulge their sympathies, a case better calculated to excite them can scarcely be imagined. A people, once numerous, powerful, and truly independent, found by our ancestors in the quiet and uncontrolled possession of an ample domain, gradually sinking beneath our superior policy, our arts and our arms, have yielded their lands, by successive treaties, each of which contains a solemn guarantee of the residue, until they retain no more of their formerly extensive territory than is deemed necessary to their comfortable subsistence. To preserve this remnant, the present application is made.

Before we can look into the merits of the case, a preliminary inquiry presents itself. Has this court jurisdiction of the cause? The third article of the constitution describes the extent of the judicial power. The second section closes an enumeration of the cases to which it is extended, with "controversies between a state or citizens thereof, and foreign states, citizens or subjects." A subsequent clause of the same section gives the supreme court original jurisdiction, in all cases in which a state shall be a party. The party defendant may then unquestionably be sued in this court. May the plaintiff sue in it? Is the Cherokee nation a foreign state, in the sense in which that term is used in the constitution? The counsel for the plaintiffs have maintained the affirmative of this proposition with great earnestness and ability. So much of the argument as was intended to prove the character of the Cherokees as a state, as a distinct political society, separated from others, capable of managing its own affairs and governing itself, has in the opinion of a majority of the judges, been completely successful. They have been uniformly treated as a state, from the settlement of our country. The numerous treaties made with them by the United States, recognise them as a people capable of maintaining the relations of peace and war, of being responsible in their political character for any violation of their engagements, or for any aggression committed on the citizens of the United States, by any individual of their community. Laws have been enacted in the spirit of these treaties. The acts of our government plainly recognise the Cherokee nation as a state, and the courts are bound by those acts.

A question of much more difficulty remains. Do the Cherokees constitute a foreign state in the sense of the constitution? The counsel have shown conclusively, that they are not a state of the Union, and have insisted that, individually, they are aliens, not owing allegiance to the United States. An aggregate of aliens composing a state must, they say, be a foreign state; each individual being foreign, the whole must be foreign.

This argument is imposing, but we must examine it more closely, before we yield to it. The condition of the Indians in relation to the United States is, perhaps, unlike that of any other two people in existence. In general, nations not owing a common allegiance, are foreign to each other. The term foreign nation is, with strict propriety, applicable by either to the other. But the relation of the Indians to the United States is marked by peculiar and cardinal distinctions which exist nowhere else. The Indian territory is admitted to compose a part of the United States. In all our maps, geographical treaties, histories and laws, it is so considered. In all our intercourse with foreign nations, in our commercial regulations, in any attempt at intercourse between Indians and foreign nations, they are considered as within the jurisdictional limits of the United States, subject to many of those restraints which are imposed upon our own citizens. They acknowledge themselves, in their treaties, to be under the protection of the United States; they admit, that the United States shall have the sole and exclusive right of regulating the trade with them, and managing all their affairs as they think proper; and the Cherokees in particular were allowed by the treaty of Hopewell, which preceded the constitution, "to send a deputy of their choice, whenever they think fit, to congress." Treaties were made with some tribes, by the state of New York, under a then unsettled construction of the confederation, by which they ceded all their lands to that state, taking back a limited grant to themselves, in which they admit their dependence. Though the Indians are acknowledged to have an unquestionable, and heretofore unquestioned, right to the lands they occupy, until that right shall be extinguished by a voluntary cession to our government; yet it may well be doubted, whether those tribes which reside within the acknowledged boundaries of the United States can, with accuracy, be denominated foreign nations. They may, more correctly, perhaps, be denominated domestic dependent nations. They occupy a territory to which we assert a title independent of their will, which must take effect in point of possession, when their right of possession ceases. Meanwhile, they are in a state of pupilage; their relation to the United States resembles that of a ward to his guardian. They look to our government for protection: rely upon its kindness and its power; appeal to it for relief to their wants; and address the president as their great father. They and their country are considered by foreign nations, as well as by ourselves, as being so completely under the sovereignty and dominion of the United States, that any attempt to acquire their lands, or to form a political connection with them would be considered by all as an invasion of our territory and an act of hostility. These considerations go far to support the opinion, that the framers of our constitution had not the Indian tribes in view, when they opened the courts of the Union to controversies between a state or the citizens thereof and foreign states.

In considering this subject, the habits and usages of the Indians, in their intercourse with their white neighbors, ought not to be entirely disregarded. At the time the constitution was framed, the idea of appealing to an American court of justice for an assertion of right or a redress of wrong, had perhaps never entered the mind of an Indian or of his tribe. Their appeal was to the tomahawk, or to the government. This was well understood by the statesmen who framed the constitution of the United States, and might furnish some reason for omitting to enumerate them among the parties who might sue in the courts of the Union. Be this as it may, the peculiar relations between the United States and the Indians occupying our territory are such, that we should feel much difficulty in considering them as designated by the term foreign state, were there no other part of the constitution which might shed light on the meaning of these words. But we think that in construing them, considerable aid is furnished by that clause in the eighth section of the third article, which empowers congress to "regulate commerce with foreign nations, and among the several states, and with the Indian tribes." In this clause, they are as clearly contradistinguished,m by a name appropriate to themselves, from foreign nations, as from the several states composing the Union. They are designated by a distinct appellation; and as this appellation can be applied to neither of the others, neither can the application distinguishing either of the others be, in fair construction, applied to them. The objects to which the power of regulating commerce might be directed, are divided into three distinct classes-foreign nations, the several states, and Indian tribes. When forming this article, the convention considered them as entirely distinct. We cannot assume that the distinction was lost, in framing a subsequent article, unless there be something in its language to authorize the assumption.

The counsel for the plaintiffs contend, that the words "Indian tribes" were introduced into the article, empowering congress to regulate commerce, for the purpose of removing those doubts in which the management of Indian affairs was involved by the language of the ninth article of the confederation. Intending to give the whole of managing those affairs to the government about to be instituted, the convention conferred it explicitly; and omitted those qualifications which embarrassed the exercise of it, as granted in the confederation. This may be admitted, without weakening the construction which has been intimated. Had the Indian tribes been foreign nations, in the view of the convention, this exclusive power of regulating intercourse with them might have been, and most probably, would have been, specifically given, in language indicating that idea, not in language contradistinguishing them from foreign nations. Congress might have been empowered "to regulate commerce with foreign nations, including the Indian tribes, and among the several states." This language would have suggested itself to statesmen who considered the Indian tribes as foreign nations, and were yet desirous of mentioning them particularly.

It has been also said, that the same words have not necessarily the same meaning attached to them, when found in different parts of the same instrument; their meaning is controlled by the context. This is undoubtedly true. In common language, the same word has various meanings, and the peculiar sense in which it is used in any sentence, is to be determined by the context. This may not be equally true with respect to proper names. "Foreign nations" is a general term, the application of which to Indian tribes, when used in the American constitution, is, at best, extremely questionable. In one article, in which a power is given to be exercised in regard to foreign nations generally, and to the Indian tribes particularly, they are mentioned as separate, in terms clearly contradistinguishing them from each other. We perceive plainly, that the constitution, in this article, does not comprehend Indian tribes in the general term "foreign nations;" not, we presume, because a tribe may not be a nation, but because it is not foreign to the United States. When, afterwards, the term "foreign state" is introduced, we cannot impute to the convention, the intention to desert its former meaning, and to comprehend Indian tribes within it, unless the context force that construction on us. We find nothing in the context, and nothing in the subject of the article, which leads to it.

The court has bestowed its best attention on this question, and, after mature deliberation, the majority is of opinion, that an Indian tribe or nation within the United States is not a foreign state, in the sense of the constitution, and cannot maintain an action in the courts of the United States.

A serious additional objection exists to the jurisdiction of the court. Is the matter of the bill the proper subject for judicial inquiry and decision? It seeks to restrain a state from the forcible exercise of legislative power over a neighboring people, asserting their independence; their right to which the state denies. On several of the matters alleged in the bill, for example, on the laws making it criminal to exercise the usual powers of self-government in their own country, by the Cherokee nation, this court cannot interpose; at least, in the form in which those matters are presented.

That part of the bill which respects the land occupied by the Indians, and prays the aid of the court to protect their possession, may be more doubtful. The mere question of right might, perhaps, be decided by this court, in a proper case, with proper parties. But the court is asked to do more than decide on the title. The bill requires us to control the legislature of Georgia, and to restrain the exertion of its physical force. The propriety of such an interposition by the court may be well questioned; it savors too much of the exercise of political power, to be within the proper province of the judicial department. But the opinion on the point respecting parties makes it unnecessary to decide this question.

If it be true, that the Cherokee nation have rights, this is not the tribunal in which those rights are to be asserted. If it be true, that wrongs have been inflicted, and that still greater are to be apprehended, this is not the tribunal which can redress the past or prevent the future. The motion for an injunction is denied."

However, that wasn't the end of the judicial proceedings. Prior to *Cherokee Nation v. Georgia* being heard by the Supreme Court, the state of Georgia passed a law stating that Georgia residents obtain a license before settling in Cherokee territory (1830). A missionary named Samuel Austin Worcester, who lived among the Cherokee, refused to obtain the required license. State officials understood that the missionaries were sympathetic to the Cherokee resistance to the Georgia government, so Worcester and a fellow missionary were indicted, tried, and convicted by a Georgia court.

The missionaries appealed their case to the Supreme Court, and in 1832, *Worcester v. Georgia* was heard by the Court. Ruling that the Cherokee nation was a separate political entity, the Court overturned the missionaries' convictions and pointed out that only the federal government was authorized to regulate business and treaty-based negotiations conducted within the boundaries of Native American nations. Thus, the Court overturned the Georgia law on the basis of the fact that the states were not authorized to negotiate the terms of use of Native American lands.

Both the state of Georgia and President Andrew Jackson ignored the ruling. One of the quotes Jackson is best known for, "John Marshall has made his decision, now let him enforce it", is an apocryphal reference to this case. While he did not exactly say that, he did comment on the case to a friend, "The decision of the Supreme Court has fell still born, and they find that they cannot coerce Georgia to yield to its mandate." Jackson thus ignored what Marshall had written and moved ahead with the Indian Removal Act, ordering the state of Georgia to forcibly remove the Cherokee. In a stunning and dangerous break with American Constitutional law, Jackson had essentially argued that since the court had no way of enforcing its mandates, the President was free to do as he pleased.

Notable critics in Congress were outraged, including Henry Clay of Kentucky and John Quincy Adams of Massachusetts, who both thought the Act was a stain on American history. They also lambasted Jackson as an ignoramus who had no restraint or respect for the rule of law, in keeping with criticism of Jackson for being a populist. Over the course of his Presidency, critics would come to strongly detest Jackson and derisively label him "King Jackson."

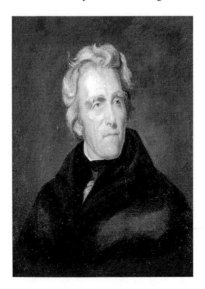

President Jackson

One of the most famous protests came in the form of a letter written in 1836 by Transcendentalist Ralph Waldo Emerson to President Van Buren. Emerson's letter illustrates the degree to which the Cherokees had successfully assimilated into American culture by the time of their removal:

> "Sir, my communication respects the sinister rumors that fill this part of the country concerning the Cherokee people. The interest always felt in the aboriginal population – an interest naturally growing as that decays – has been heightened in regard to this tribe. Even in our distant State some good rumor of their worth and civility has arrived. We have learned with joy their improvement in the social arts. We have read their newspapers. We have seen some of them in our schools and colleges. In common with the great body of the American people, we have witnessed with sympathy the painful labors of these red men to redeem their own race from the doom of eternal inferiority, and to borrow and domesticate in the tribe the arts and customs of the Caucasian race. And notwithstanding the unaccountable apathy with which of late years the Indians have been sometimes abandoned to their enemies, it is not to be doubted that it is the good pleasure and the understanding of all humane persons in the Republic, of the men and the matrons sitting in the thriving independent families all over the land, that they shall be duly cared for; that they shall taste justice and love from all to whom we have delegated the office of dealing with them."

Chapter 5: The Trail of Tears

> "The Cherokees are nearly all prisoners. They have been dragged from their houses, and encamped at the forts and military posts, all over the nation. In Georgia, especially, multitudes were allowed no time to take any thing with them except the clothes they had on. Well-furnished houses were left prey to plunderers, who, like hungry wolves, follow in the trail of the captors. These wretches rifle the houses and strip the helpless, unoffending owners of all they have on earth."[5]

Jackson's refusal to enforce the will of the Supreme Court was the catalyst that sparked a determined effort to force the Cherokee out of Georgia. On May 23, 1836, the U.S. Senate ratified the Treaty of New Echota by a single vote. This treaty allegedly existed between the Cherokee nation and the U.S. government, but no Cherokee representatives signed it. The New Echota Treaty set a two-year deadline for the voluntary exodus of all Cherokee people from their ancestral homelands; after May 23, 1838, any Cherokee remaining in their historic lands would be removed by military force. Ross reacted as one would expect to the ratification of a treaty that

---

[5] National Park Service, "The Trail of Tears and the Forces Relocation of the Cherokee Nation," http://www.nps.gov/nr/twhp/wwwlps/lessons/118trail/118facts3.htm

no Cherokees had signed:

"By the stipulations of this instrument, we are despoiled of our private possessions, the indefeasible property of individuals. We are stripped of every attribute of freedom and eligibility for legal self-defence. Our property may be plundered before our eyes; violence may be committed on our persons; even our lives may be taken away, and there is none to regard our complaints. We are denationalized; we are disfranchised. We are deprived of membership in the human family! We have neither land nor home, nor resting place that can be called our own. And this is effected by the provisions of a compact which assumes the venerated, the sacred appellation of treaty... The instrument in question is not the act of our Nation; we are not parties to its covenants; it has not received the sanction of our people. The makers of it sustain no office nor appointment in our Nation, under the designation of Chiefs, Head men, or any other title, by which they hold, or could acquire, authority to assume the reins of Government, and to make bargain and sale of our rights, our possessions, and our common country. And we are constrained solemnly to declare, that we cannot but contemplate the enforcement of the stipulations of this instrument on us, against our consent, as an act of injustice and oppression, which, we are well persuaded, can never knowingly be countenanced by the Government and people of the United States; nor can we believe it to be the design of these honorable and highminded individuals, who stand at the head of the Govt., to bind a whole Nation, by the acts of a few unauthorized individuals. And, therefore, we, the parties to be affected by the result, appeal with confidence to the justice, the magnanimity, the compassion, of your honorable bodies, against the enforcement, on us, of the provisions of a compact, in the formation of which we have had no agency."

Nevertheless, the United States Secretary of War, Lewis Cass, explained the treaty to Chief John Ross by simply saying that President Jackson no longer recognized the existence of any governmental organization among the Eastern Cherokee and thus had no obligation to uphold previous treaties. Also, no one would be allowed to challenge the legitimacy of the treaty.

General John Ellis Wool was the commander first assigned the task of disarming and removing those Cherokee unwilling to depart from their ancestral homelands voluntarily. Upon arriving in Cherokee territory, Wool and his command were greeted by a group of Cherokee leaders who presented him with a signed memorial countering the treaty's terms for both removal and disarmament, and in September 1836, Wool attended a council where he learned about the Cherokee opinion toward the Treaty of New Echota. The general would later write that "not one [of the Cherokee]…would receive either rations or clothing from the United States lest they might compromise themselves in regard to the treaty." Convinced that the treaty was neither moral nor legal, Wool asked to be relieved of his command, a practically unheard of act by a commanding officer. He was promptly relieved and replaced by General Winfield Scott.

Wool

Meanwhile, Brigadier General Richard G. Dunlap and his Tennessee troops began building the stockades that would house the Cherokee en route to their new homes in the Oklahoma territory, as well as barracks to house the troops that would guard the Cherokee along the way. By the time authorities were done, over 30 "forts" had been built to house the Cherokee in North Carolina, Georgia, Alabama, and Tennessee before forcing them west. However, in the course of building these structures, Dunlap and his men met and spoke with Cherokee people, and they also became convinced that the sophistication of the Cherokee, many of whom had converted to Christianity and were well educated, did not deserve the treatment they would meet in the crude wooden pens built for their virtual imprisonment. Believing that continuing with his orders would compromise the honor of his men, Dunlap, like General Wool before him, threatened to resign his commission. In response, President Jackson ordered a cessation of all communication with Cherokee leader John Ross.

By August 1837, the state of Georgia had outlawed meetings by the Cherokee Council, so thousands of Cherokee people began to gather at Red Clay, Tennessee, which they adopted as the new seat of Cherokee government. A U.S. government representative sent expressly to convince the Cherokee to comply with the Treaty of New Echota offered only a message indicating that resistance was futile. A British witness to the meetings named George Featherstonhaugh would later reflect upon the accommodation the Cherokee had made toward assimilation and comment:

"a whole Indian nation abandons the pagan practices of their ancestors, adopts the

Christian religion, uses books printed in their own language, submits to the government of their elders, builds houses and temples of worship, relies upon agriculture for their support, and produces men of great ability to rule over them...Are not these the great principles of civilization? They were driven from their religious and social state then, not because they cannot be civilized, but because a pseudo set of civilized beings who are too strong for them want their possessions!"

Nevertheless, the Indian Removal Act of 1830 had called for the forced removal of all tribes east of the Mississippi River, and the Trail of Tears began in earnest in May 1838. The removal itself was both physically violent and emotionally devastating. Spouses were often separated from one another, children were torn from their parents, and looters ended up stealing the possessions that the Cherokees could not round up fast enough before their removal.

The Cherokees were forced along three separate trails that utilized both overland and water routes and averaged about 1,200 miles. The forced removal was carried out by some 7,000 federal troops, and those Cherokee people who refused to comply voluntarily with the removal order (about 15% of the estimated 15,000-20,000 Cherokees forced west) were herded at bayonet point into prepared collection points.

As the first three groups left in the summer of 1838 from Chattanooga, they were supposed to be moved by rail, boat, and wagon along what was designated as the "Water Route". However, the river levels were so low that it proved impossible to navigate them, forcing one group to travel by land across Arkansas. Due to illness and a summer drought, that group averaged 3-5 deaths daily.

Meanwhile, 15,000 other Cherokees remained prisoners, and the overcrowding and poor sanitation led to so many illnesses and deaths that the Cherokees still in the east actually requested that they not be forced to move until the fall. Although that request was accepted, the Cherokees were forced to remain in the camps, continuing to suffer the depredations and misery of the natural conditions.

In November, a dozen groups consisting of 1,000 Cherokees each began the trek west, and most of the groups had to endure traveling 800 miles by land. Only one party, which included Principal Chief Ross, traveled by water. This time, too much rain made the roads so muddy that they became impassable, slowing down the forced marches, and the lack of grazing ground did not support the animals that could have been used for food.

As a result, the forced relocation completely bogged down, and about 10,000 of the Cherokees found themselves freezing during the winter months while still east of the Mississippi. One of the survivors would later note, "Long time we travel on way to new land. People feel bad when they leave Old Nation. Womens cry and make sad wails. Children cry and many men cry...but they say nothing and just put heads down and keep on go towards West. Many days pass and people die very much." Another survivor noted that each new day brought the death of a family member, until his parents and five siblings were all gone: "One each day. Then all are gone."

Of course, the Cherokees weren't the only ones forced to endure the weather, since they were being guarded by thousands of soldiers. After Wool had refused the assignment, Winfield Scott assumed command of the Georgia troops charged with moving the Cherokee off of their land. From the beginning, Scott, commonly known as "Old Fuss and Feathers," rightly feared that the Georgia troops would rather kill the Native Americans than see them safely to the "Indian Territory" in present-day Oklahoma.

Sure enough, the Georgia troops treated the Native Americans in a barbaric manner. One Georgia volunteer, who would later become a Confederate Colonel during the Civil War, described the removal of the Cherokee as "the cruelest work I ever knew." This comment came from a man who later saw his own soldiers "shot to pieces" during Civil War battles. One missionary, who had been working among the Cherokee at the time of the removal and chose to travel west with them, said that the removal was conducted without any humane treatment of the Native Americans and that General Scott's orders were largely ignored. In a letter written in January 1839, Lucy Ames Butler, the wife of a missionary among the Cherokees, noted:

"My husband has been engaged in camp, preaching and attending on the sick Cherokees, since they were first taken. He was appointed to serve as Physician in one of the first companies. He also preaches in camp on the Sabbath as they have made arrangements not to travel on that day. We have heard from several companies, and understand they have considerable sickness. Twenty-five in a company of seven hundred had died, when they had proceeded three hundred miles. In another, which numbered about the same, in two hundred miles, eighteen had been laid in their graves. I have not heard particularly from others. When these companies arrive in their new country, the greatest part will be without shelters as they were in this [place], after they were prisoners; and it is to be feared many will be cut down by death, as has been the case with new emigrants in the country. It is estimated about two thousand died while in camp in this country.

Will not the people in whose power it is to redress Indian wrongs awake to their duty? Will they not think of the multitudes among the various tribes that have within a few years been swept into Eternity by the cupidity of the 'white man' who is in the enjoyment of wealth and freedom on the original soil of these oppressed Indians? I know many friends of the Indians have set down in despair, thinking oppression has been carried so far, nothing now can be done. I will mention one person who thinks otherwise; and it may surprise you when I tell it is John Ross, the principal Chief of these oppressed Cherokees. In speaking of the distresses of his people, I have heard him with subdued agitation of feeling, with calmness and confidence say, 'Though for years, the Press has been closed against us, and the few friends we have left, have at times, been ready to think we must sink to ruin unheard; yet I cannot think the United States' Government is so lost to all justice, that our wrongs will not be redressed, if the truth is fairly set before those, who have the power to do it.'

With these feelings, this man has presented himself at our seat of Government year after year; and though false reports, in almost every form, have been circulated against him, and indignities heaped on him and his associates, and withal being told by the highest Authorities of our Government, that he must accept [the] terms already offered, that nothing more favourable would ever be granted, yet the returning Congress has again found him at Washington pleading for his people. It may now be thought as his people have actually been driven from their native country, and one eighth of them already cut off by death, that he will think nothing can be gained by further intercession; but probably, if his life is spared, he will again be seen pleading with Government, for those that remain."

As that letter noted, Chief Ross, who had so fervently opposed the forced removal, had tragically found himself in charge of an event that would result in the deaths of over one-third of his people. In the end, Ross would leave his homeland with the last of 13 groups of Cherokee in December of 1838, carrying with him the tribe's laws and historical records. Before his arrival in the Oklahoma Territory in late March of 1839, Ross would bury his own wife in a shallow grave along the trail, and she joined an estimated 8,000 other Cherokees in death. Nonetheless, in March 1839, Ross dutifully reported:

Dear Sir,

We would respectfully inform you that we arrived here on yesterday the 14th Inst & that we are here and do not know what dis-position to make of the public Teams & of the public property in our charge. We have no funds to pay for the Subsistence of the teams & the waggoners & we wish some immediate instructions on the subject. The Agent of the Government will be here today. We will be mustered out of Service and Turned Over to government & we are informed that they have some shelled corn & Some very poor beef for our Subsistence which is unfit for use & from the promises made to us in the Nation East we did not Expect such treatment.

Very Respectfully

Mr John Ross Your Most Obt Sevts

George Hicks &

Collins McDonald

Today the forced removal of the Cherokee is poignantly and somberly remembered as the "Trail of Tears", and in the Cherokee language the event was known as "Nunahi-Duna-Dlo-Hilu-I" ("The Trail Where They Cried"). To a great extent, the incident can be viewed as a predictive event signaling the subsequent course relations between Native Americans and the United States would take. The forced removal is also indicative of the attitudes toward Native Americans held by famed "Indian fighters" like Andrew Jackson and William Henry Harrison. As the President of the United States, Jackson's actions demonstrated his disdain for both the Supreme Court and those who disagreed with his vision for the United States. Also, Jackson's policy toward Native Americans changed the policies of previous presidents, who had encouraged Native Americans to assimilate and thereby become "civilized". Perversely, Jackson's attitudes and actions toward Native American punished those tribes that had achieved the highest levels of assimilation, and although Jackson had left office by the time of the Cherokee removal, his Vice-President and successor, Martin Van Buren, vowed to continue Jackson's policies and appointed all but one of Jackson's cabinet members to serve him as well.

The Cherokee Trail of Tears was not the first incident of forced removal in North America, but their removal had profound effects. Immediately prior to the Cherokee removal, the Choctaw, Chickasaw, and Creek Nations all elected to leave their traditional homelands, though they did so under extreme duress. But with the Cherokee's forced removal, assimilation, which had been the official policy of the U.S. government, was effectively abandoned. Instead, the forced removal of Native Americans from their traditional homelands effectively became U.S. government policy. In the second half of the 19th century, the Navajo people of the American Southwest were forced from their land in an incident they refer to as the Long Walk. Several tribes on the Great Plains, like the Sioux, resisted in a series of wars but ultimately suffered the same fate.

Chapter 6: The Removal of the Creek

By the mid-1820s, the Creek, like dozens of other Native American groups, were among those targeted for removal to reservations west of the Mississippi River. This process had actually begun decades earlier with President Thomas Jefferson listing "Indian Removal" as part of the reason for the Louisiana Purchase, but the Lower Creek had mistakenly interpreted their friendly status with the U. S. as excluding them from the process. In 1825, Secretary of War John Calhoun proposed that negotiations begin with the Chickasaw and Creek, and the federal government renewed negotiations with the remaining Cherokee and Choctaw, the majority of which had already accepted relocation or had been forcibly driven west. Calhoun stated, "No arrangement ought to be made which does not regard the interest of the Indians as well as our own . . ." He further urged, "There are to be the strongest and the most solemn assurance that the country given them should be theirs, as a permanent home for themselves and their posterity, without being disturbed by the encroachment of our citizens."[6]

---

[6]   *Green, Donald E.* The Creek People. *Page 38.*

Between 1818 and 1830, the Creek would sign a number of treaties with the U.S. until virtually all their land holdings had been given away, including the Treaty of Fort Mitchell (in 1818), Treaty(ies) of Indian Springs (in 1821 and 1825), Treaty of Washington (in 1826), and Treaty of the Creek Indian Agency (in 1827). William McIntosh was the primary signer of the second Indian Springs Treaty, and when word spread that he had taken a $25,000 bribe to cede the remaining Creek lands in Georgia and Alabama, he was assassinated.

Portrait of William McIntosh

In 1829, Andrew Jackson addressed the Creek and told them:

"Friends and Brothers – By permission of the Great Spirit above, and the voice of the people, I have been made President of the United States, and now speak to you as your Father and friend, and request you to listen. Your warriors have known me long You know I love my white and red children, and always speak with a straight, and not with a forked tongue; that I have always told you the truth ... Where you now are, you and my white children are too near to each other to live in harmony and peace. Your game is destroyed, and many of your people will not work and till the earth. Beyond the great River Mississippi, where a part of your nation has gone, your Father has provided a country large enough for all of you, and he advises you to remove to it. There your white brothers will not trouble you; they will have no claim to the land, and you can live upon it you and all your children, as long as the grass grows or the water runs, in peace and plenty. It will be yours forever. For the improvements in the country where you now live, and for all the stock which you cannot take with you, your Father will pay you a fair price..."

On May 28, 1830, President Andrew Jackson signed a bill giving his agents broad discretionary power to force Creek leaders to sign removal treaties and compel Creek citizens to vacate to a point west of the Mississippi River. But even after substantively resigning themselves to relocation, of the more than 21,000 Creek in question, only 630 actually made the journey west, with the others resigning themselves and accepting allotments of their own land and conforming to white laws.

However, even as Creek and U.S. representatives were in the final stages of land negotiation, settlers and Creek groups engaged in violence. In one location where the Creek had erected a village along the Lower Chatahoochee River, settlers staged a violent raid, forcing the Creek off their land, burning down their houses, and then erecting their own buildings so as to claim the village as their own. This continued in village after village to such an extent that by 1833, and countless homeless bands of Creek were wandering the countryside, foraging just to stay alive. To make matters worse, unscrupulous land agents targeted abandoned land allotments, paying unprincipled natives a few dollars to sign away rights to land they didn't even own. Since "Indians" could not testify in American courts, neither could they be prosecuted nor forced to prove their identity. And while some agents of the U. S. Government tried to protect Creek rights, there simply weren't enough Army troops or volunteers willing to defend them against fellow Americans.

Things would come to a head a few years later with the so-called "Second Creek War." By 1836, the remaining Creek had endured all they could. Roving bands of starving Creek destroyed cabins, burned crops and barns, and killed white settlers, sending those who survived streaming into Columbus, Georgia for protection. Soon after, a toll bridge was burned, a stagecoach was robbed, and two steamboats on the Chattahoochee River were captured. Local law enforcement officers sided with the settlers, but to Alabama Governor Clement Clay, the picture was clear: "It seems to me that the opinion prevails extensively, if not universally, that the frauds and forgeries practiced upon the Indians to deprive them of their lands, were amongst the principal causes which excited them to hostilities."[7]

By the summer of 1836, Upper Creek leaders prompted by *Opothle Yahola* organized a force of about 1,800, and they joined an estimated 9,000 whites dedicated to ending all hostilities in the region once and for all. As a result, by July the renegade Creek had either surrendered to U. S. authorities, been killed, or joined their Seminole and Creek brethren in the Florida swamps. Hundreds, including Lower Creek leader *Eneah Emathla*, were placed in leg-irons and led to Fort Mitchell, Alabama. By July 14, more than 2,000 Creek had been marched the 90 miles to Montgomery, the first leg of their forced relocation to a reservation west of the Mississippi River. Another 2,500 Creek were forced aboard steamships headed down the Alabama River. As a journalist of the time wrote, "To see the remnant of a once mighty people fettered and chained together forced to depart from land of their fathers into a country unknown to them, is of itself sufficient to move the stoutest heart"[8]

Over the next several months, between the summer of 1836 and spring of 1837, 14,000 Creek made a 1200 mile journey over the span of three months, traveling 800 miles on foot and 400 miles by boat to their new assigned territory. Though assured they would first be given ample time to sell their homes and arrange for transport of their possessions, that seldom proved the case. The Creek warriors had chosen to remain behind to keep the federal government from seizing their homes as "abandoned" were ultimately drawn into the Seminole War raging in Florida and thus considered hostiles. As a result, even the most prosperous of "loyal" Creek arrived in "Indian Territory" (Oklahoma) with only what they could carry on their backs. In an unsigned letter received by the Army officer assigned to seeing to the logistics of the move, a Creek had written, "You have heard the cries of our women and children. Our road has been a long one . . . and on it we have laid the bones of our men, women and children. We wanted to gather our crops and we wanted to go in peace and friendship. Did we? No! We were drove off like wolves!"[9] Ultimately, an estimated 3,500 Creek were buried along the "Removal Trail," with 40% of the remaining population lost to disease, inability to complete the journey, or decision to make a go of it on their own shortly after arrival.

For the vast majority of Creek arriving via the "Removal Trail," settling in on the reservation proved more difficult than for many other indigenous populations. While those who had arrived voluntarily and brought tools and livestock certainly had their share of obstacles, for groups like the Creek who came with little more than the clothes on their backs, adaptation was secondary to simple survival. Even so, soon after arrival they organized themselves into work parties, set up temporary lodges (sticks covered with bark or skin) and set to clearing fields, often using only *tomahawks* or crudely-fashioned hoes. Furthermore, tensions were still high between Upper and

---

[7]   *Green, Donald E.* The Creek People. *Page 47.*

[8]   *James, Michael. "The Birthplace Of Osceola."*

[9]   *Green, Donald E.* The Creek People. *Page 49.*

Lower Creek, so there was initially little cooperation as the Lower Creek settled along the Arkansas and Verdigris rivers where the Upper Creek had established themselves.

While the new environment spelled imminent change for the Creek, the first cultural casualty of this adaptive process was the loss of spiritual stability. Although the new towns that sprang up were named after former Creek *idalwas* for a sense of cultural continuity, traditional *chokofas* (council meeting places) and *chunkey* yards were not included. As a result, families increasingly decided to live independently away from the town proper. Additionally, although relatively few Creek had converted to Christianity prior to the move, due to "sexual misconduct" perpetrated by a Methodist missionary accused of coercing a young Creek girl into having sex, the Creek Council made it a punishable offense to attend Christian church. As a result, schisms developed between traditional Creek, converted Creek who would sneak onto the Cherokee Nation to attend Christian services, and those who believed spirituality was an individual choice. The no-church ban was lifted by 1840, but by then the three spiritually-based factions had already chosen courses independent of one another, which greatly undermined Creek Nation cohesion. This division was further exacerbated when faction members were required to recognize leaders who did not share their religion or spiritual persuasion.

From 1840-1860, the Creek Council's most important function and greatest challenge proved to be writing the Creek Code of Law and Creek Constitution. While other indigenous groups had opted by-and-large to adopt versions of the U.S. Constitution, the Creek observe societal practices far different than both Americans and other Native American groups. On one level, they were ahead of American society in allowing Creek women to own and control property apart from that of their husbands, but they also condoned slavery. Slavery had existed prior to European contact, and it became more mainstream with the introduction of Southern plantation life. Much like American law, if a Creek killed a slave, he was required to compensate the slave owner, but if a slave killed a Creek, he was summarily put to death. Similarly, marriage and sex was strictly prohibited between Creek and blacks, with any such violators sentenced to death. While the Creek Nation itself had acquired a small number of slaves to help maintain communal fields, Creek leaders like Benjamin Marshall, Benjamin Perryman, and Roley McIntosh owned hundreds to operate their huge cotton plantations. Under Creek law, some free blacks held relatively important positions as interpreters, artisans, and advisers on trade matters.

Although the Treaty of Fort Gibson (1833) had expanded the land originally allotted the Creek by giving them lands formerly part of the Cherokee Nation, it also gave the Seminole the legal right to settle Creek land as well. The Lower Creek had intermingled with the Seminole to such an extent during the previous century that many Creek claimed both Creek and Seminole tribe membership. However, it wasn't until the Third Seminole War (1855-1858) that most Seminole finally resigned themselves to reservation life. Thus, while the Seminole were recognized as kin, growing Creek nationalism increasingly viewed the Seminole as competitors. In an effort to remain separate, in 1856 the Creek Nation ceded land between the Canadian and North Canadian rivers to the Seminole.

When word reached the Creek Nation in 1861 that shots fired at Fort Sumter, South Carolina would likely result in yet another war, there was little concern because they figured the Civil War would take place half a continent away. Unbeknownst to them, their land would be deemed part of the South and thus turn them into enemies. Accordingly, within weeks, Federal monies were discontinued, Federal troops were withdrawn, and "Indian Territory" fell under control of the new Confederate government. Suddenly, the future of the Creek Nation was more precarious than at any time since European arrival, and factioning that had already established divisions among the Creek intensified as other indigenous nations chose sides. The Chickasaw and Choctaw allied with the South, while the Creek, Seminole, and Cherokee jockeying for position based on the outcome they anticipated.

About half the male Creek population participated in the Civil War, but throughout the fighting, the splintering Creek factions became more clearly defined, resulting in what many historians term the "New Creek Civil War". This was a series of battles involving followers of *Opothle Yahola* and Principal Chief Motey Canard, culminating in guerrilla warfare at the Cherokee Outlet at Chustenalah on December 26, 1861. That resulted in about 6,500 Creek and Seminole loyal to the Union being driven into exile in Kansas.

Tragically, even though the Creek/Seminole contingency represented the greatest supporters of the Union during the Civil War among the Native American population, after the war was over, the federal government declared that they had broken the agreements contained in the removal treaties. According to the U.S., they therefore relinquished any rights guaranteed them under those treaties. This began a new process of treaty negotiation between the Creek and the federal government.

Late in 1865, the Creek and Seminole hiding in Kansas returned to Oklahoma to begin the rebuilding process, but upon their arrival, they found their homes burned, their cattle gone, and their fields full of weeds. The federal government used this opportunity to exert Federal control, seizing a major portion of Creek land by taking over 3 million acres in the western portion of the reservation. The government then sold a portion of that land to the Seminole Nation for 50 cents per acre. On June 14, 1866, government officials presented the Creek with the particulars of the new treaty they would be compelled to sign. The stipulations included the abolition of slavery, the permitting of non-Creek freedmen to become Creek citizens, and allowance of two railroads to be built and assume right-of-way directly through the heart of Creek lands.

After floundering aimlessly for nearly a year, the various Creek factions decided it was in their best interest to reestablish unity and draw up a new constitution that would provide them the best defense against further interference. Formally declaring themselves the "Muscogee Nation," a new document was drawn up by mid-1867 providing for a National Council comprised of a lower House of Warriors and upper House of Kings, with each town electing a representative to the House of Kings. There was also a Principal and Second chief modeled after the president and vice president, and the entire Nation was divided into six judicial districts, with judges chosen by the National Council. Additionally, police (called "lighthorse"), prosecuting attorneys, and a court system were established. Since the Creek traditionally did not favor imprisonment, when a man was arrested, he was chained to a tree, and men found guilty were typically branded or whipped. Those committing more serious crimes were punished by death, usually by firing squad.

The new government chose a site on their original council grounds at Hitchitee as their capital, and by 1878 a two-story stone structure was constructed. On August 18, 1885, the "Great Seal of the Muscogee Nation I.T." was designed and issued for all official documents.

Despite these efforts, the Creek people lost their traditional roots shortly after the Civil War. Most leaders were of mixed blood, and a century or more of interaction with other tribes and white settlers had diluted their traditional culture. Even though towns remained centers for traditional festivals like the Green Corn Dance, they lost most of their religious and cultural significance except for a minority of elders and traditionalists. Christianity also gradually became part of the fabric of Creek culture, and it was nearly predominant by 1870. This paved the way for new missions to be accepted in Creek territory, including Baptists and then Presbyterians, who also established new schools. White missionaries helped start 31 day schools by 1871; and 70 day schools and 6 boarding schools by 1896.

Most Creek eventually adapted to the new soil, but independent living now amounted to individually-owned log cabins surrounded by numerous outbuildings like barns, chicken coops, sheds, and enclosed animal pens. The Creek managed as many acres of farmland as they could, but most reservation land was also leased out to various cattlemen enterprises, with 61 companies and wealthy individuals leasing over 1 million acres of Creek land to graze their cattle. This helped propel the Creek Nation on its way to unprecedented prosperity. To expand on their economic options, in 1867 the Creek started cooperating with the neighboring Cherokee Nation, and then all of the " Five Civilized Tribes" (Cherokee, Chickasaw, Choctaw, Creek, and Seminole) the following year. The Creek Nation even established a publication, *Indian Journal*, to announce their positions on various issues and keep their people informed. As the end of the 19th century was approaching, the Creek had not only taken the dominant progressive role among the local co-op, they had also extended offers of friendship to the neighboring Plains Indians.

Unfortunately, things took a drastic turn for the worse. In 1877, the federal government enacted a bill that would once again put the future of the Muskogee (Creek) Nation in jeopardy. As the culmination of several bills designed to break up a number of Indian reservations, the Dawes Act required members of several indigenous groups to accept individual allotments of land, a prelude to preparing Oklahoma Territory for statehood and opening huge sections of land to settlers. Then, in what would become known as the "Great Land Rush," on April 22, 1889 some 2 million acres of settled and unsettled land was opened to settlers to buy. In 1893, a Federal Commission approached the Muskogee about pulling up stakes once again in exchange for individual land ownership rather than national ownership. In opposition, the Muskogee united under Principal Chief Isparhecher, a conservative leader who vocally opposed the idea of distributing Muskogee assets among individuals he described as "ill-equipped to retain them."

On June 28, 1898 the final blow was delivered when the Curtis Act made tribal governments illegal, rendering Chief Isparhecher and every other tribal leader powerless outside the Nation and answerable to the federal government. Henceforth, the Creek Council could make laws as they chose, but they had to be approved by the President of the United States. The Muskogee Nation attempted to test the U.S. resolve by passing a law providing funds to fight on the grounds that it violated their former treaty, which President McKinley summarily vetoed.

Chapter 7: The Seminole Wars

In the early 19th century, the United States turned its attention to removal of the Muscogee and numerous other Native American groups of the Southeast, intending to relocate them to specially-designated areas beyond the Mississippi River. To address the growing insurgency of Native Americans amassing in Florida, which now included members of other indigenous groups and hundreds of escaped slaves, General Andrew Jackson invaded Florida with a makeshift army in 1818. Jackson declared the "Indian issue" under control by the following year. Depending upon the source, by some reckoning the First Seminole War actually lasted from 1814-1819.

Almost immediately after the British ceded Florida to the United States in 1819, the American government began urging the Seminole to sell their lands and join the other "tribes" moving to "Indian Territory." However, as soon as it was realized that the Florida Seminole intended to resist relocation, plans for a second war were put into motion.

On May 26, 1830, Andrew Jackson signed into law the Indian Removal Act of 1830. 2 years later, the Treaty of Cusseta compelled the Creek Nation to cede all Muscogee lands east of the Mississippi River to the U. S. Government. Through the Indian Removal Act and the Treaty of Cusseta, Creek tribal leaders were to exchange the last of the Muscogee ancestral homelands for land allotments in the newly-designated "Indian Territory" west of the Mississippi in Oklahoma. This came just five years after the 1827 Treaty of Cession, which included this language:

> "the [Lower Creek] Chiefs and head men aforesaid, agree to cede, and they do hereby cede to the United States, all the remaining lands now owned or claimed by the Creek Nation . . . within the chartered limits of the State of Georgia. In consideration whereof, and in full compensation . . . the United States, do hereby agree to pay to the Chiefs and head men of the Creek Nation the sum of twenty-seven thousand four hundred and ninety-one dollars. It is further agreed . . . [that] the additional sum of fifteen thousand dollars, it being the understanding of both the

parties, that five thousand dollars of this sum shall be applied . . . towards the education and support of Creek children at the school in Kentucky, known by the title of the "Chocktaw [sic] Academy."

While part of the Lower Creek people voluntarily gave up their homeland claims and became known as one of the "Five Civilized Tribes", other members refused to recognize the treaty and joined their relatives in the Florida Everglades. Many of the Lower Creeks had already joined their Seminole brethren two decades earlier and fought in the First Seminole War. Now they were on the brink of a second such confrontation.

An 1835 sketch of a Seminole village, indicating that they lived in log cabins.

While there are many conflicting accounts regarding what actually ignited the Second Seminole War, according to one commonly-accepted report, a number of settlers had fled to Fort King (in present-day Ocala, Florida) after an estimated 300 Seminoles attacked several plantations and a militia wagontrain in mid-1835. In response, two companies of U. S. Army soldiers and militia, numbering 110 soldiers under the command of Major Francis L. Dade, were sent from Fort Brooke to reinforce Fort King. On December 28, members of a Seminole band ambushed the soldiers, slaughtering all but two. Over the next few months, Generals Clinch, Gaines, and Winfield Scott, as well as territorial governor Richard Keith Call, led large numbers of troops across the state in futile pursuit of those responsible. While the Seminole managed to elude capture, they also attacked several more isolated farms, settlements, plantations, and U. S.

Army forts. They even burned the Cape Florida lighthouse.

An 1837 portrait of Seminole Chief Coeehajo

From 1836-1838, the U. S. Army instituted the forced removal of more than 20,000 natives from the Southeast to the new "Indian Territory", but about 300 Seminole managed to evade capture by hiding in Florida's jungles. Some also disappeared into the swamps of the Everglades. By February of 1836, the Seminole and their escaped slave allies had attacked 21 plantations along the river in Flagler County on Florida's east coast. Late that same year, U. S. Quartermaster Major General Thomas Jesup was placed in command of the war and quickly instituted a strategy aimed at concentrating the Army's energies on wearing down the Seminole rather than sending out large patrols to track them down. The Army had learned far too often that soldiers could easily be ambushed on patrol.

Jesup

With more than 9000 men under his command, Jesup maintained patrols of the coast, inland rivers and streams. By January of 1837, his efforts began to pay off. Seminole casualties were reaching a critical point, prompting several Seminole chiefs to send messengers asking to arrange a truce. By March a "Capitulation" agreement had been signed by several chiefs, including the leading Seminole War Chief Micanopy, stipulating that for willingly accepting removal to "Indian Territory," they could be accompanied by their allies and the slaves with them. By the end of May 1837, several chiefs (including Micanopy) had surrendered to U. S. authorities, prompting Jesup to declare the Second Seminole War an American victory. But two very powerful Seminole war chiefs, Osceola and Ar-pi-uck-i (also known as Sam Jones), were vehemently opposed to relocation and intended to continue resisting.

An 1825 painting of Micanopy by Charles Bird King

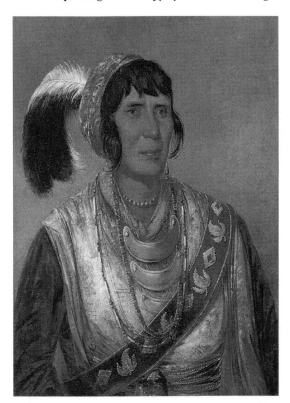

1838 painting of Osceola by George Catlin

On June 2, 1837, Osceola, Ar-pi-uck-i and about 200 followers entered the poorly-protected holding camp at Fort Brooke in present-day Tampa, and they managed to free the 700 Seminole natives in captivity. On Jesup's orders, Brigadier General Joseph Marion Hernández then invited several Seminole chiefs, including Coacoochee ("Wild Cat"), John Horse, Osceola, and Micanopy, to a conference under a white flag of truce. When they arrived, however, they were all promptly taken into custody and imprisoned. Coacoochee and John Horse managed to escape, but Osceola would die in his Fort Marion cell in St. Augustine, probably of malaria.

With Jesup and his troops slowly forcing the Seminole ever southward, the Second Seminole War dragged on for five more years, a game of cat-and-mouse resulting in a number of casualties on both sides as various Seminole factions effectively evaded capture.

In May 1841, Colonel William J. Worth assumed command of U. S. Army forces in Florida and immediately ordered his men on a search-and-destroy mission geared at rounding up the Seminole in north Florida's jungles. Ultimately, some Seminole chose to surrender to avoid starvation, while others were seized when they came in to negotiate surrender, including Coacoochee for a second time. According to some accounts, Coacoochee was bribed to give up and persuade others to do likewise.

Finally convinced that the remaining Seminole posed no real danger, in 1842 Colonel Worth recommended that those still free be left in peace. He subsequently received authorization to leave the remaining Seminole on an informal reservation in southwestern Florida. With the Second Seminole War declared officially over on August 14, 1842, by the end of that year the remaining Native Americans (including some of the Seminole) living outside the reservation were rounded up and driven west. By April 1843, the U. S. Army presence in Florida had been reduced to one regiment, and that November Worth reported that only about 95 Seminole men and 200 women and children still remained in Florida. With such paltry numbers, Worth told authorities that the Seminole were no longer a threat.

Worth

While there is no official record of the number of Seminole killed during the Second Seminole War, there is no doubt that hundreds of natives died of disease, starvation or battle. Many more died on the long journey west or died soon after reaching the new "Indian Territory." The removal of the Seminole is considered part of the "Trail of Tears", in which an estimated 100,000 Native Americans living between Michigan, Louisiana, and Florida were forcibly moved west. That number included 46,000 Muscogee Creek, Seminole, Cherokee, Chickasaw, and Choctaw. Thousands of Native Americans, many of whom were transported hundreds of miles in chains, died of disease, exposure to the elements, starvation, or execution. An estimated 3500 Alabama Creek died alone.

After a period of adjustment in the new "Indian Territory," the Lower Muscogee Creek and newly-arriving Seminole established farms and plantations on the Arkansas and Verdigris rivers, while the Upper Muscogee reestablished traditional towns on the Canadian River and its northern branches. With both groups routinely sending representatives to a National Council that met near High Springs, Florida, the Muscogee Creek Nation began to recover their heritage and experience new prosperity. And while Florida governmental agencies continued to press for the forced removal of all Native Americans across the state, the Seminole stayed close to the reservation for the most part and intentionally avoided contact with whites. Only occasionally would groups of 10 or so men visit Tampa to trade.

In 1845, Thomas P. Kennedy, an entrepreneur who operated a store at Fort Brooke on Tampa Bay, converted his fishing station on nearby Pine Island into a trading post for the Native Americans. It did not do well, however. Americans who routinely sold whiskey to the Seminole told them that if they patronized Kennedy's store, they would be captured and sent west. When the trading post subsequently burned down in 1848, most assumed it was done by a band of Native Americans known to be living outside the reservation. This band was referred to as "outsiders", and it consisted of about 20 warriors led by a renegade called Chipco. The group included seven Mikasuki, six Seminole, a Creek, and a Yuchi.

Unprepared to reignite hostilities with the Seminole, the U.S. Army sent Major General David E. Twiggs to Florida and called up two companies of mounted volunteers to guard settlements. But in August 1850 an orphan boy living on a farm in north central Florida was apparently killed by Native Americans, and the federal government decided to seek a more permanent solution. In 1851, the U. S. Secretary of the Interior appointed General Luther Blake to forcibly remove the last remaining Native Americans of Florida.

Unable to implement a decisive plan, Blake was replaced with Captain Casey in 1853. Casey initially attempted a diplomatic approach by trying to convince the Seminole to move west, but the chiefs refused. In August 1854, Secretary of War Jefferson Davis initiated a program to force the Seminole into a final conflict. Davis' plan included a trade embargo, the survey and sale of Seminole land in southern Florida to European prospectors, and a stronger U. S. Army presence to protect the new white settlers. Davis said that if the Seminole did not agree to leave voluntarily, the Army would use force. This set the stage for yet another bloody confrontation.

On December 7, 1855 First Lieutenant George Hartsuff, who had led previous patrols, left Fort Myers on Florida's west coast with 10 men and two wagons. Hartsuff would later report finding no Seminole while en route, but he did pass cornfields and three deserted Seminole villages, including that of Seminole leader Holata Micco (also known as "Billy Bowlegs"). On the morning of December 20, 1855, while loading their wagons to prepare for the return trip back to Fort Myers, 40 Seminole led by Holata Micco attacked the army camp and shot several soldiers, including Lieutenant Hartsuff. The Seminole reportedly killed and scalped four men in the camp, killed the wagon mules, looted and burned the wagons, and left with several horses. Seven men, including Hartsuff, managed to make their way back to Fort Myers.

A portrait of Holata Micco

When news of the attack reached Tampa, militia officers were elected and companies were organized. Secretary of War Jefferson Davis accepted two infantry companies and three mounted companies, totaling about 260 men. Florida Governor James E. Broome kept another 400 men mobilized and *on alert* under state control. But as the Tampa *Herald* would later report, the "mounted troops usually made their patrols in open country where it was easier to travel but where they could be seen by the Seminoles." This made the American soldiers easy to pick-off or avoid.

On January 6, 1856, two men gathering coontie weed (also known as Florida arrowroot and wild sago) south of the Miami River were killed by Seminole raiders, prompting area settlers to flee to Forts Dallas and Key Biscayne. Then a party of about 20 Seminole attacked a wood-cutting patrol outside Fort Denaud, killing five. Even though militia units were positioned specifically to defend the Tampa Bay area, the Seminole also successfully raided the coast just south of Tampa, killing one man and burning a house in present-day Sarasota. And on March 31, 1856, the Seminole attacked the "Braden Castle", the plantation home of Dr. Joseph Braden in what is now Bradenton.

But two days after a Seminole band attacked a farm two miles from Fort Meade, 20 militia from Fort Fraser caught a Seminole patrol by surprise along Peace River and killed 20.

According to the Seminole account, only four warriors were killed, but this included War Chief Ocsen Tustenuggee, who was apparently the only chief willing to lead attacks against white settlements.

In September 1856, Brigadier General William S. Harney returned to Florida as commander of all the federal troops stationed there. Remembering lessons he had learned about fighting the Seminole during the Second Seminole War, he set up a line of forts across Florida from where he could send patrols deep into Seminole territory. In mid-1857, 10 additional companies of Florida militia were mustered into federal service, bringing the number to nearly 800 men by September. They subsequently captured 18 women and children from Holata Micco's band and burned several Seminole towns and their fields.

On March 15, 1858, Holata Micco and Chief Assunwha accepted a cash offer of $500 per warrior (more for chiefs) and $100 per woman to relocate west. On May 4, 1858 a total of 163 Seminole were transported to New Orleans and then taken to Oklahoma. Four days later, Colonel Gustavus Loomis, the commander of the Department of Florida, declared the Third Seminole War over.

Chapter 8: The Aftermath for the Cherokee

The total death toll of the Indian Removal Act is somewhere between 5,000-25,000, but the Cherokees tried to rebuild their institutions over the next several decades after the Trail of Tears. Nevertheless, when the Curtis Act of 1898 dismantled all tribal governments and institutions ahead of admitting the federal territory where the Cherokees had been relocated into new states, it eliminated he Cherokee courts and government in the region yet again.

Having already lost their land, the Cherokees were also deprived of their unique identity during the end of the 19th century when the South went about instituting Jim Crow laws. By implementing a segregated society, the Native Americans were naturally categorized as colored, meaning they were treated no better than African Americans. Until the Civil Rights Movement helped secure basic civil rights for minorities, the Cherokees suffered right alongside everyone else.

Today the federal government currently recognizes three distinct bands of Cherokee people. These are the Cherokee Nation of Oklahoma, United Keetoowah Band of Cherokee Indians (Oklahoma), and the Eastern Band of Cherokee Indians (North Carolina). A fourth band, the Echota Cherokee, located in northern Alabama, is recognized only by that state.

Among Native American tribes today, the Cherokee is the second largest in terms of registration of official tribal members and boasts some 300,000 tribal citizens. A 7,000 square mile plot in eastern Oklahoma is home to about 70,000 Cherokee and is not a reservation but rather a federally-recognized sovereign nation. The Cherokee Nation functions with a governmental system similar to that of the United States and includes judicial, executive and legislative branches.

Despite everything they endured, the Cherokee tribe has continued to assimilate to the extent of their abilities. In 1976, the Cherokee Nation drafted and approved a new constitution that allotted executive power to a Principal Chief who is elected to four-year terms by registered tribal voters. The legislative power of the tribe rests with the Tribal Council, presided over by a Deputy Principal Chief who functions in this way much like the Vice President of the United States in his role over the Senate. The Cherokee Nation Appeals Tribunal holds the judicial power within the nation and includes a District Court and the Tribal Appeals Tribunal, which function very much like U.S. District Courts and the Supreme Court respectively. These courts hear cases brought before them based on the Cherokee Nation Judicial Code.

The Cherokee Nation has overcome severe obstacles and setbacks, but the tribe has repeatedly proven that its people are resilient and resourceful. In the modern era, the tribe has overcome discrimination and hardship to establish themselves as not only a successful Native American tribe but as an economically and politically viable entity, fully capable of self-government and self-determination. The tribe has established business ventures and has successfully established a tax system independent of the United States. The Cherokee Nation stands as a model not only for other Native American tribes but for citizens in general, as their resourcefulness and shrewd political acumen has afforded them the chance to thrive in the 21st century.

Chapter 9: The Aftermath for the Creek and Seminole

The Seminole Wars were disastrous for the Seminole, but the American Civil War may have been the single greatest misfortune for the Muscogee Creek. Despite the fact it wasn't their war, the Creek, Seminole, and Cherokee ultimately suffered far greater losses than whites in any part of the United States, losing a greater percentage of their populations than any Southern or Northern state.

Most tribes initially remained neutral, but once Union forces were withdrawn from forts south of the Mason-Dixon Line, federal annuities guaranteed by various treaties were discontinued. Most Indian agents sided with the South, making it sensible for the Native Americans to aid the Confederacy as much as possible.

In March of 1861, at an intertribal council, the Seminole let it be known that they were not inclined to sign a treaty with the Confederacy. But after American attorney and Confederate officer Albert Pike pointed out that federal annuities guaranteed by various treaties would be discontinued, Seminole Chief John Jumper agreed to raise a few men. Jumper ultimately raised just 46, but Union officer Sumner C.H. Carruth recognized the possibility that thousands of Native Americans might help the Confederacy. He reported to his commanders, "The Indians will make no further resistance to the south until help is furnished them, while a little aid would thoroughly arouse the union feeling. Before spring, they must either be our enemies or friends."

In mid-1861, Creek and Seminole leaders signed a treaty with the Confederacy (as did the Cherokee, Choctaw, and Catawba) that committed their warriors to defense of the South. The Seminole would ultimately fight in numerous battles, but only after one last futile attempt at peace. In August of 1861, after discovering that Muscogee Creek and Seminole leaders had formally committed their people to the Confederacy, a speaker for the council of Upper Creeks named Opothleyahola gathered an estimated 4000-5000 Creek and Seminole on his ranch in the Indian Territory. He convinced them they must avoid getting involved in the "White Man's War", even if it meant uprooting their families and seeking freedom in a northern state.

Opothleyahola

Hoping President Lincoln would support their "peace" cause, Opothleyahola wrote a letter asking for federal protection. He pleaded:

> "Now I write to the President our Great Father who removed us to our present homes and made a treaty, and you said that in our new homes we should be defended from all interference from any person and that no white people in the whole world should ever molest us . . . and should we be injured by any body you would come with your soldiers and punish them. But now the wolf has come, men who are strangers tread our soil. Our children are frightened and the mothers cannot sleep for fear."

By April 1863, the nearly 8000 Creek and Seminole receiving supplies from the Union Army in Kansas decided to fight for the North. With peace no long a viable possibility, Creek, Seminole, and a large number of escaped slaves with them volunteered to form one of the first colored regiments in the Civil War. Since most Native Americans did not speak English, the escaped slaves who were with them often served as interpreters.

Fighting their way to Kansas, this regiment participated in the first three battles taking place in "Indian Territory," with the official organization and mustering of the First Indian Regiment taking place in May of 1862. Thus, by the end of the Civil War, the Creek, Seminole, and other related groups had fought on both the Union and Confederate sides.

Nevertheless, the most critical blow came on September 8, 1865, at a conference held at Fort Smith in Arkansas. The conference was held to address the state of Indian Affairs, and commissioner Dennis N. Cooley announced, "The following named tribes have by their own acts, by making treaties with the enemies of the United States at the dates hereafter named, forfeited all rights to annuities, lands, and protection of the United States." Listing 12 tribes, including the Creek and Seminole, Cooley continued, " . . . [these tribes] are left with no treaty whatever or treaty obligations for protection by the United States."

Thus, the future of the Muscogee (Creek and Seminole) people was more uncertain than ever.

According to the Reconstruction Treaty of 1866, the Muscogee Creek Nation was required to cede 3.2 million acres, approximately half their territory, to the United States. After the Seminole Nation agreed to the Treaty, the tribal council elected John Frippo Brown, a Seminole of the Tiger Clan who had been a Confederate Army officer during the War, as the last principal chief of the Seminole Nation. Brown would also serve as "governor" of the tribe from 1885-1901 and from 1905-1906, when the tribal government was abolished in preparation for formally admitting the State of Oklahoma into the Union.

The members of the Florida Seminole who accepted reservation lands and adapted to the American system are today federally recognized as the "Seminole Tribe of Florida." Similarly, those members who prefer the more traditional lifestyle are now federally recognized as the "Miccosukee Tribe of Indians of Florida." Those Seminole not affiliated with either of the federally-recognized groups are known as the "Traditional" or "Independent Seminole", but they do not hold federal recognition. Although the language is thought to be extinct among the Oklahoma Seminole, most members of the Florida Nation speak the Miccosukee language, which is also spoken by the Miccosukee Tribe. Some Seminole have maintained the Creek language, particularly on the Brighton Reservation. In the census taken in 2000, there were approximately 2,000 enrolled members, with over 1,300 living on the reservations.

There is also a second large contingent of Seminole people in Oklahoma today. Located in Seminole County, Oklahoma, the Native American population there is 22% of the total county population. The Seminole Nation of Oklahoma is headquartered in Wewoka, the county seat. Seminole County, which covers approximately 633 square miles, is essentially a checkerboard of Indian allotments, restricted Indian lands, tribal trust property, and dependent Indian communities, with the latest figures indicating a "service" population of 5,315 Seminole residents and a total enrollment of the Seminole Nation numbering over 17,000.

Eyewitness John Burnett's Account of the Trail of Tears

"Children: This is my birthday, December 11, 1890, I am eighty years old today. I was born at Kings Iron Works in Sulllivan County, Tennessee, December the 11th, 1810. I grew into manhood fishing in Beaver Creek and roaming through the forest hunting the deer and the wild boar and the timber wolf. Often spending weeks at a time in the solitary wilderness with no companions but my rifle, hunting knife, and a small hatchet that I carried in my belt in all of my wilderness wanderings.

On these long hunting trips I met and became acquainted with many of the Cherokee Indians, hunting with them by day and sleeping around their camp fires by night. I learned to speak their language, and they taught me the arts of trailing and building traps and snares. On one of my long hunts in the fall of 1829, I found a young Cherokee who had been shot by a roving band of hunters and who had eluded his pursuers and concealed himself under a shelving rock. Weak from loss of blood, the poor creature was unable to walk and almost famished for water. I carried him to a spring, bathed and bandaged the bullet wound, and built a shelter out of bark peeled from a dead chestnut tree. I nursed and protected him feeding him on chestnuts and toasted deer meat. When he was able to travel I accompanied him to the home of his people and remained so long that I was given up for lost. By this time I had become an expert rifleman and fairly good archer and a good trapper and spent most of my time in the forest in quest of game.

The removal of Cherokee Indians from their lifelong homes in the year of 1838 found me a young man in the prime of life and a Private soldier in the American Army. Being acquainted with many of the Indians and able to fluently speak their language, I was sent as interpreter into the Smoky Mountain Country in May, 1838, and witnessed the execution of the most brutal order in the History of American Warfare. I saw the helpless Cherokees arrested and dragged from their homes, and driven at the bayonet point into the stockades. And in the chill of a drizzling rain on an October morning I saw them loaded like cattle or sheep into six hundred and forty-five wagons and started toward the west.

One can never forget the sadness and solemnity of that morning. Chief John Ross led in prayer and when the bugle sounded and the wagons started rolling many of the children rose to their feet and waved their little hands good-by to their mountain homes, knowing they were leaving them forever. Many of these helpless people did not have blankets and many of them had been driven from home barefooted.

On the morning of November the 17th we encountered a terrific sleet and snow storm with freezing temperatures and from that day until we reached the end of the fateful journey on March the 26th, 1839, the sufferings of the Cherokees were awful. The trail of the exiles was a trail of death. They had to sleep in the wagons and on the ground without fire. And I have known as many as twenty-two of them to die in one night of pneumonia due to ill treatment, cold, and exposure. Among this number was the beautiful Christian wife of Chief John Ross. This noble hearted woman died a martyr to childhood, giving her only blanket for the protection of a sick child. She rode thinly clad through a blinding sleet and snow storm, developed pneumonia and died in the still hours of a bleak winter night, with her head resting on Lieutenant Greggs saddle blanket.

I made the long journey to the west with the Cherokees and did all that a Private soldier could do to alleviate their sufferings. When on guard duty at night I have many times walked my beat in my blouse in order that some sick child might have the warmth of my overcoat. I was on guard duty the night Mrs. Ross died. When relieved at midnight I did not retire, but remained around the wagon out of sympathy for Chief Ross, and at daylight was detailed by Captain McClellan to assist in the burial like the other unfortunates who died on the way. Her unconfined body was buried in a shallow grave by the roadside far from her native home, and the sorrowing Cavalcade moved on.

Being a young man, I mingled freely with the young women and girls. I have spent many pleasant hours with them when I was supposed to be under my blanket, and they have many times sung their mountain songs for me, this being all that they could do to repay my kindness. And with all my association with Indian girls from October 1829 to March 26th 1839, I did not meet one who was a moral prostitute. They are kind and tender hearted and many of them are beautiful.

The only trouble that I had with anybody on the entire journey to the west was a brutal teamster by the name of Ben McDonal, who was using his whip on an old feeble Cherokee to hasten him into the wagon. The sight of that old and nearly blind creature quivering under the lashes of a bull whip was too much for me. I attempted to stop McDonal and it ended in a personal encounter. He lashed me across the face, the wire tip on his whip cutting a bad gash in my cheek. The little hatchet that I had carried in my hunting days was in my belt and McDonal was carried unconscious from the scene.

I was placed under guard but Ensign Henry Bullock and Private Elkanah Millard had both witnessed the encounter. They gave Captain McClellan the facts and I was never brought to trial. Years later I met 2nd Lieutenant Riley and Ensign Bullock at Bristol at John Roberson's show, and Bullock jokingly reminded me that there was a case still pending against me before a court martial and wanted to know how much longer I was going to have the trial put off?

McDonal finally recovered, and in the year 1851, was running a boat out of Memphis, Tennessee.

The long painful journey to the west ended March 26th, 1839, with four-thousand silent graves reaching from the foothills of the Smoky Mountains to what is known as Indian territory in the West. And covetousness on the part of the white race was the cause of all that the Cherokees had to suffer. Ever since Ferdinand DeSoto made his journey through the Indian country in the year 1540, there had been a tradition of a rich gold mine somewhere in the Smoky Mountain Country, and I think the tradition was true. At a festival at Echota on Christmas night 1829, I danced and played with Indian girls who were wearing ornaments around their neck that looked like gold.

In the year 1828, a little Indian boy living on Ward creek had sold a gold nugget to a white trader, and that nugget sealed the doom of the Cherokees. In a short time the country was overrun with armed brigands claiming to be government agents, who paid no attention to the rights of the Indians who were the legal possessors of the country. Crimes were committed that were a disgrace to civilization. Men were shot in cold blood, lands were confiscated. Homes were burned and the inhabitants driven out by the gold-hungry brigands.

Chief Junaluska was personally acquainted with President Andrew Jackson. Junaluska had taken 500 of the flower of his Cherokee scouts and helped Jackson to win the battle of the Horse Shoe, leaving 33 of them dead on the field. And in that battle Junaluska had drove his tomahawk through the skull of a Creek warrior, when the Creek had Jackson at his mercy.

Chief John Ross sent Junaluska as an envoy to plead with President Jackson for protection for his people, but Jackson's manner was cold and indifferent toward the rugged son of the forest who had saved his life. He met Junaluska, heard his plea but curtly said, "Sir, your audience is ended. There is nothing I can do for you." The doom of the Cherokee was sealed. Washington, D.C., had decreed that they must be driven West and their lands given to the white man, and in May 1838, an army of 4000 regulars, and 3000 volunteer soldiers under command of General Winfield Scott, marched into the Indian country and wrote the blackest chapter on the pages of American history.

Men working in the fields were arrested and driven to the stockades. Women were dragged from their homes by soldiers whose language they could not understand. Children were often separated from their parents and driven into the stockades with the sky for a blanket and the earth for a pillow. And often the old and infirm were prodded with bayonets to hasten them to the stockades.

In one home death had come during the night. A little sad-faced child had died and was lying on a bear skin couch and some women were preparing the little body for burial. All were arrested and driven out leaving the child in the cabin. I don't know who buried the body.

In another home was a frail mother, apparently a widow and three small children, one just a baby. When told that she must go, the mother gathered the children at her feet, prayed a humble prayer in her native tongue, patted the old family dog on the head, told the faithful creature good-by, with a baby strapped on her back and leading a child with each hand started on her exile. But the task was too great for that frail mother. A stroke of heart failure relieved her sufferings. She sunk and died with her baby on her back, and her other two children clinging to her hands.

Chief Junaluska who had saved President Jackson's life at the battle of Horse Shoe witnessed this scene, the tears gushing down his cheeks and lifting his cap he turned his face toward the heavens and said, "Oh my God, if I had known at the battle of the Horse Shoe what I know now, American history would have been differently written."

At this time, 1890, we are too near the removal of the Cherokees for our young people to fully understand the enormity of the crime that was committed against a helpless race. Truth is, the facts are being concealed from the young people of today. School children of today do not know that we are living on lands that were taken from a helpless race at the bayonet point to satisfy the white man's greed.

Future generations will read and condemn the act and I do hope posterity will remember that private soldiers like myself, and like the four Cherokees who were forced by General Scott to shoot an Indian Chief and his children, had to execute the orders of our superiors. We had no choice in the matter.

Twenty-five years after the removal it was my privilege to meet a large company of the Cherokees in uniform of the Confederate Army under command of Colonel Thomas. They were encamped at Zollicoffer and I went to see them. Most of them were just boys at the time of the removal but they instantly recognized me as "the soldier that was good to us". Being able to talk to them in their native language I had an enjoyable day with them. From them I learned that Chief John Ross was still ruler in the nation in 1863. And I wonder if he is still living? He was a noble-hearted fellow and suffered a lot for his race.

At one time, he was arrested and thrown into a dirty jail in an effort to break his spirit, but he remained true to his people and led them in prayer when they started on their exile. And his Christian wife sacrificed her life for a little girl who had pneumonia. The Anglo-Saxon race would build a towering monument to perpetuate her noble act in giving her only blanket for comfort of a sick child. Incidentally the child recovered, but Mrs. Ross is sleeping in a unmarked grave far from her native Smoky Mountain home.

When Scott invaded the Indian country some of the Cherokees fled to caves and dens in the mountains and were never captured and they are there today. I have long intended going there and trying to find them but I have put off going from year to year and now I am too feeble to ride that far. The fleeing years have come and gone and old age has overtaken me. I can truthfully say that neither my rifle nor my knife were stained with Cherokee blood.

I can truthfully say that I did my best for them when they certainly did need a friend. Twenty-five years after the removal I still lived in their memory as "the soldier that was good to us".

However, murder is murder whether committed by the villain skulking in the dark or by uniformed men stepping to the strains of martial music.

Murder is murder, and somebody must answer. Somebody must explain the streams of blood that flowed in the Indian country in the summer of 1838. Somebody must explain the 4000 silent graves that mark the trail of the Cherokees to their exile. I wish I could forget it all, but the picture of 645 wagons lumbering over the frozen ground with their cargo of suffering humanity still lingers in my memory.

Let the historian of a future day tell the sad story with its sighs, its tears and dying groans. Let the great Judge of all the earth weigh our actions and reward us according to our work.

Children - Thus ends my promised birthday story. This December the 11th 1890."

Bibliography

Finger, John R. Cherokee Americans: The Eastern Band of Cherokees in the 20th century. Knoxville: University of Tennessee Press, 1991.

Irwin, L, "Cherokee Healing: Myth, Dreams, and Medicine." American Indian Quarterly. Vol. 16, 2, 1992, p. 237.

McLoughlin, William G. Cherokee Renascence in the New Republic. (Princeton: Princeton University Press, 1992).

Mooney, James. "Myths of the Cherokees." Bureau of American Ethnology, Nineteenth Annual Report, 1900, Part I. pp. 1–576. Washington: Smithsonian Institution.

Perdue, Theda. "Clan and Court: Another Look at the Early Cherokee Republic." American Indian Quarterly. Vol. 24, 4, 2000, p. 562.

Perdue, Theda. Cherokee women: gender and culture change, 1700–1835. Lincoln: University of Nebraska Press, 1999.

Rollings, Willard H. "The Osage: An Ethnohistorical Study of Hegemony on the Prairie-Plains." (University of Missouri Press, 1992)

Made in the USA
Middletown, DE
28 November 2014